The Rise of Universities

—— THE ——

RISE OF UNIVERSITIES

By *Charles Homer Haskins*

Cornell Paperbacks

Cornell University Press

ITHACA AND LONDON

PREFATORY NOTE

CHARLES HOMER HASKINS was born in Meadville, Pennsylvania, on December 21, 1870. He laid the foundations of his thorough mastery of languages, both ancient and modern, and of his vast scholarship at a remarkably young age. When five or six years old, he was taught Latin, and shortly afterwards Greek, by his father. He graduated from The Johns Hopkins University at the age of sixteen and then studied in Paris and Berlin. He acquired his doctor's degree and started teaching at Johns Hopkins when not yet twenty. After twelve years at the University of Wisconsin, Haskins was called to Harvard University in 1902 and taught there until the year 1931, when ill health compelled him to retire. He died in Cambridge on May 14, 1937.

In the course of his long association with Harvard, Haskins became one of the great men of that university, not merely in his position as Dean of the Graduate School of Arts and Sciences from 1908 to 1924 but above all because of the power of his personality. No more succinct testimony can be found than the sketch of the basic traits of Haskins' character which was drawn by three of his closest colleagues at the time of his death:

Vigorous and progressive in his method of teaching history both as a liberal art and as a humane science, a sovereign influence on all advanced students of history, since all took one or more of his courses, powerful in Faculty debates, unravelling Gordian knots as quickly as others could cut them, marked out for a college president from the start, though not tempted by several important invitations to such an office, witty and gay in conversation, fond of long walks, a favorite at his clubs, best of friends, deeply reverential and religious at heart, he made himself immediately one of the indispensables in the life of Harvard and left a name to be recorded among its greatest.[1]

Haskins' gifts as an eminently able administrator and man of affairs extended his influence far

[1] Quoted from the obituary note in *Speculum*, XIV (1939), 414, which was composed by R. P. Blake, G. R. Coffman, and E. K. Rand.

beyond Harvard. Throughout his active life he played a leading role in many of the important scholarly organizations of this country, including the American Historical Association, the Mediaeval Academy of America, and the American Council of Learned Societies. At the end of the First World War he served with distinction on the American Peace Delegation in Paris as chairman of the Division of Western Europe.

In his own scholarly work Haskins concentrated on the era of the High Middle Ages from the eleventh to the thirteenth century. One of his earliest interests was the study of the institutions of northern France. On the basis of the most meticulous archival investigations he published finally, in 1918, his *Norman Institutions*, which took its place as a standard work in the history of the French and English institutions of the period. The other wide field of Haskins' interests was the development of thought and learning, and within this field he gave particular attention to the history of science during the High Middle Ages. His thorough acquaintance with the great European manuscript collections enabled him to draw on hitherto unused material and thus to throw entirely new light on the many and highly variegated problems discussed by him in a large number of articles. The most important results of these life-long researches Haskins brought together in two collections of essays: *Studies in the History of Science* (1924; 2nd ed., 1927) and *Studies in Mediaeval Culture* (1929). But besides these monographic studies he composed also a highly stimulating synthesis in his book *The Renaissance of the Twelfth Century* (1927), which ever since its publication has appealed to a wide circle of readers.

As his friend F. M. Powicke remarked, "Haskins preferred to be his own 'popularizer.'" [2] Thus he discussed the significance of *The Normans in European History* in a series of lectures at Harvard and at the University of California, published under that title in 1925. Likewise he summarized his views on *The Rise of Universities* in three lectures at Brown University in 1923 and thereby provided a work which has remained unsurpassed in the conciseness and vividness of its account.

In 1929, in celebration of the fortieth anniversary of the beginning of his teaching career, there appeared a large volume of *Anniversary Essays in Mediaeval History by Students of Charles Homer Haskins*. Among the contributors we find not a few names of scholars who in their turn were to become outstanding in the field of mediaeval history and whose widespread interests and creative work reflect

[2] See F. M. Powicke's article on Haskins in the *English Historical Review*, LII (1937), 653.

the inspiration and the training which they once received from their master.

Since Haskins represents the rare case of a man who combined the qualities of the efficient organizer, the original scholar, and the great teacher, it can be said "without exaggeration," in the words of a prominent French mediaevalist, F. Jouon des Longrais, that "Charles Homer Haskins was truly the soul of the renascence of mediaeval studies in the United States."

THEODOR E. MOMMSEN

Cornell University

PUBLISHER'S NOTE: Except for a few minor changes which bring certain references up to date, the text of these lectures is identical with that of the 1923 edition. Several footnotes, however, have been added and others have been revised; the Bibliographical Note has been edited as indicated in that section.

CONTENTS

I

THE EARLIEST UNIVERSITIES

UNIVERSITIES, like cathedrals and parliaments, are a product of the Middle Ages. The Greeks and the Romans, strange as it may seem, had no universities in the sense in which the word has been used for the past seven or eight centuries. They had higher education, but the terms are not synonymous. Much of their instruction in law, rhetoric, and philosophy it would be hard to surpass, but it was not organized into the form of permanent institutions of learning. A great teacher like Socrates gave no diplomas; if a modern student sat at his feet for three months, he would demand a certificate, something tangible and external to show for it—an excellent theme, by the way, for a Socratic dialogue. Only in the twelfth and thirteenth centuries do there emerge in the world those features of organized education with which we are most familiar, all that machinery of instruction represented by faculties and colleges and courses of study, examinations and commencements and academic degrees. In all these matters we are the heirs and successors, not of Athens and Alexandria, but of Paris and Bologna.

The contrast between these earliest universities and those of today is of course broad and striking. Throughout the period of its origins the mediaeval university had no libraries, laboratories, or museums, no endowment or buildings of its own; it could not possibly have met the requirements of the Carnegie Foundation! As an historical text-book from one of the youngest of American universities tells us, with an unconscious touch of local color, it had "none of the attributes of the material existence which with us are so self-evident." The mediaeval university was, in the fine old phrase of Pasquier, "built of men"—*bâtie en hommes.* Such a university had no board of trustees and published no catalogue; it had no student societies—except so far as the university itself was fundamentally a society of students—no college journalism, no dramatics, no athletics, none of those "outside activities" which are the chief excuse for inside inactivity in the American college.

And yet, great as these differences are, the fact remains that the university of the twentieth century is the lineal descendant of mediaeval Paris and Bologna. They are the rock whence we were hewn; the hole of the pit whence we were digged. The fundamental organization is the same, the historic continuity is unbroken. They created the university tradition of the modern world, that common tradition which belongs to all our institutions of higher learning, the newest as well as the oldest, and which all college and university men should know and cherish. The origin and nature of these earliest universities is the subject of these three lectures. The first will deal with university institutions, the second with university instruction, the third with the life of university students.

In recent years the early history of universities has begun to attract the serious attention of historical scholars, and mediaeval institutions of learning have at last been lifted out of the region of myth and fable where they long lay obscured. We now know that the foundation of the University of Oxford was not one of the many virtues which the millennial celebration could properly ascribe to King Alfred; that Bologna did not go back to the Emperor Theodosius; that the University of Paris did not exist in the time of Charlemagne, or for nearly four centuries afterward. It is hard, even for the modern world, to realize that many things had no founder or fixed date of beginning but instead "just grew," arising slowly and silently without definite record. This explains why, in spite of all the researches of Father Denifle [1] and Hastings Rashdall [2] and the local antiquaries, the beginnings of the oldest universities are obscure and often uncertain, so that we must content ourselves sometimes with very general statements.

The occasion for the rise of universities was a great revival of learning, not that revival of the fourteenth and fifteenth centuries to which the term is usually applied, but an earlier revival, less known though in its way quite as significant, which historians now call the renaissance of the twelfth century. So long as knowledge was limited to the seven liberal arts of the early Middle Ages, there could be no universities, for there was nothing to teach beyond the bare elements of grammar, rhetoric, logic, and the still barer notions of arithmetic, astronomy, geometry, and music, which did duty for an academic curriculum. Between 1100 and 1200, however, there came a great influx of new knowledge into western Europe, partly through Italy

[1] H. Denifle, *Die Enstehung der Universitäten des Mittelalters bis 1400*, vol. I (Berlin, 1880).

[2] H. Rashdall, *The Universities of Europe in the Middle Ages*, 2 vols. in 3 (Oxford, 1895); rev. ed., 3 vols. (Oxford, 1936). Later references to this book are to the 1936 edition.

and Sicily, but chiefly through the Arab scholars of Spain—the works of Aristotle, Euclid, Ptolemy, and the Greek physicians, the new arithmetic, and those texts of the Roman law which had lain hidden through the Dark Ages. In addition to the elementary propositions of triangle and circle, Europe now had those books of plane and solid geometry which have done duty in schools and colleges ever since; instead of the painful operations with Roman numerals—how painful one can readily see by trying a simple problem of multiplication or division with these characters—it was now possible to work readily with Arabic figures; in the place of Boethius, the "Master of them that know" became the teacher of Europe in logic, metaphysics, and ethics. In law and medicine men now possessed the fulness of ancient learning. This new knowledge burst the bonds of the cathedral and monastery schools and created the learned professions; it drew over mountains and across the narrow seas eager youths who, like Chaucer's Oxford clerk of a later day, "would gladly learn and gladly teach," to form in Paris and Bologna those academic gilds which have given us our first and our best definition of a university, a society of masters and scholars.

To this general statement concerning the twelfth century there is one partial exception, the medical university of Salerno. Here, a day's journey to the south of Naples, in territory at first Lombard and later Norman, but still in close contact with the Greek East, a school of medicine had existed as early as the middle of the eleventh century, and for perhaps two hundred years thereafter it was the most renowned medical centre in Europe. In this "city of Hippocrates" the medical writings of the ancient Greeks were expounded and even developed on the side of anatomy and surgery, while its teachings were condensed into pithy maxims of hygiene which have not yet lost their vogue—"after dinner walk a mile," etc. Of the academic organization of Salerno we know nothing before 1231, and when in this year the standardizing hand of Frederick II regulated its degrees Salerno had already been distanced by newer universities farther north. Important in the history of medicine, it had no influence on the growth of university institutions.

If the University of Salerno is older in time, that of Bologna has a much larger place in the development of higher education. And while Salerno was known only as a school of medicine, Bologna was a many-sided institution, though most noteworthy as the centre of the revival of the Roman law. Contrary to a common impression, the Roman law did not disappear from the West in the early Middle Ages, but its influence was greatly diminished as a result of the Germanic invasions. Side by side with the Germanic codes, Roman law survived as the customary law of the Roman population, known no longer through the great law books of Justinian but in elementary manuals and form-books which grew thinner and more jejune as time went on. The *Digest*, the most important part of the *Corpus Juris Civilis*, disappears from view between 603 and 1076; only two manuscripts survived; in Maitland's phrase, it "barely escaped with its life." Legal study persisted, if at all, merely as an apprenticeship in the drafting of documents, a form of applied rhetoric. Then, late in the eleventh century, and closely connected with the revival of trade and town life, came a revival of law, foreshadowing the renaissance of the century which followed. This revival can be traced at more than one point in Italy, perhaps not first at Bologna, but here it soon found its centre for the geographical reasons which, then as now, made this city the meeting-point of the chief routes of communication in northern Italy. Some time before 1100 we hear of a professor named Pepo, "the bright and shining light of Bologna"; by 1119 we meet with the phrase *Bononia docta*. At Bologna, as at Paris, a great teacher stands at the beginning of university development. The teacher who gave Bologna its reputation was one Irnerius, perhaps the most famous of the many great professors of law in the Middle Ages. Just what he wrote and what he taught are still subjects of dispute among scholars, but he seems to have fixed the method of "glossing" the law texts upon the basis of a comprehensive use of the whole *Corpus Juris*, as contrasted with the meagre epitomes of the preceding centuries, fully and finally separating the Roman law from rhetoric and establishing it firmly as a subject of professional study. Then, about 1140, Gratian, a monk of San Felice, composed the *Decretum* which became the standard text in canon law, thus marked off from theology as a distinct subject of higher study; and the pre-eminence of Bologna as a law school was fully assured.

A student class had now appeared, expressing itself in correspondence and in poetry, and by 1158 it was sufficiently important in Italy to receive a formal grant of rights and privileges from Emperor Frederick Barbarossa, though no particular town or university is mentioned. By this time Bologna had become the resort of some hundreds of students, not only from Italy but from beyond the Alps. Far from home and undefended, they united for mutual protection and assistance, and this organization of foreign, or Transmontane, students was the beginning of the university. In this union they seem to have followed the example of the gilds already common in Italian cities. Indeed, the word university means originally such a group or corporation in general, and only in time did it come to be limited to gilds of masters and students, *universitas societas magistrorum discipulorumque*. Historically, the word university has no connection with the universe or the universality of learning; it denotes only the totality of a group, whether of barbers, carpenters, or students did not matter. The students of Bologna organized such a university first as a means of protection against the townspeople, for the price of rooms and necessaries rose rapidly with the crowd of new tenants and consumers, and the individual student was helpless against such profiteering. United, the students could bring the town to terms by the threat of departure as a body, secession, for the university, having no buildings, was free to move, and there are many historic examples of such migrations. Better rent one's rooms for less than not rent them at all, and so the student organizations secured the power to fix the prices of lodgings and books through their representatives.

Victorious over the townsmen, the students turned on "their other enemies, the professors." Here the threat was a collective boycott, and as the masters lived at first wholly from the fees of their pupils, this threat was equally effective. The professor was put under bond to live up to a minute set of regulations which guaranteed his students the worth of the money paid by each. We read in the earliest statutes (1317)

[9]

that a professor might not be absent without leave, even a single day, and if he desired to leave town he had to make a deposit to ensure his return. If he failed to secure an audience of five for a regular lecture, he was fined as if absent—a poor lecture indeed which could not secure five hearers! He must begin with the bell and quit within one minute after the next bell. He was not allowed to skip a chapter in his commentary, or postpone a difficulty to the end of the hour, and he was obliged to cover ground systematically, so much in each specific term of the year. No one might spend the whole year on introduction and bibliography! Coercion of this sort presupposes an effective organization of the student body, and we hear of two and even four universities of students, each composed of "nations" and presided over by a rector. Emphatically Bologna was a student university, and Italian students are still quite apt to demand a voice in university affairs. When I first visited the University of Palermo I found it just recovering from a riot in which the students had broken the front windows in a demand for more frequent, and thus less comprehensive, examinations. At Padua's seventh centenary in May 1922 the students practically took over the town, with a programme of processions and ceremonies quite their own and an amount of noise and tumult which almost broke up the most solemn occasions and did break the windows of the greatest hall in the city.

Excluded from the "universities" of students, the professors also formed a gild or "college," requiring for admission thereto certain qualifications which were ascertained by examination, so that no student could enter save by the gild's consent. And, inasmuch as ability to teach a subject is a good test of knowing it, the student came to seek the professor's license as a certificate of attainment, regardless of his future career. This certificate, the license to teach (*licentia docendi*), thus became the earliest form of academic degree. Our higher degrees still preserve this tradition in the words master (*magister*) and doctor, originally synonymous, while the French even have a *licence*. A Master of Arts was one qualified to teach the liberal arts; a Doctor of Laws, a certified teacher of law. And the ambitious student sought the degree and gave an inaugural lecture, even when he expressly disclaimed all intention of continuing in the teaching profession. Already we recognize at Bologna the standard academic degrees as well as the university organization and well-known officials like the rector.

Other subjects of study appeared in course of time, arts, medicine, and theology, but Bologna was preeminently a school of civil law, and as such it became the model of university organization for Italy, Spain, and southern France, countries where the study of law has always had political and social as well as merely academic significance. Some of these universities became Bologna's competitors, like Montpellier and Orleans as well as the Italian schools nearer home. Frederick II founded the University of Naples in 1224 so that the students of his Sicilian kingdom could go to a Ghibelline school at home instead of the Guelfic centre in the North. Rival Padua was founded two years earlier as a secession from Bologna, and only in 1922, on the occasion of Padua's seven-hundredth anniversary, I saw the ancient feud healed by the kiss of peace bestowed on Bologna's rector amid the encores of ten thousand spectators. Padua, however, scarcely equalled Bologna in our period, even though at a later age Portia sent thither for legal authority, and though the university still shines with the glory of Galileo.

In northern Europe the origin of universities must be sought at Paris, in the cathedral school of Notre-Dame. By the beginning of the twelfth century in France and the Low Countries learning was no longer confined to monasteries but had its most active centres in the schools attached to cathedrals, of which the most famous were those of Liège, Rheims, Laon,

Paris, Orleans, and Chartres. The most notable of these schools of the liberal arts was probably Chartres, distinguished by a canonist like St. Ives and by famous teachers of classics and philosophy like Bernard and Thierry. As early as 991 a monk of Rheims, Richer, describes the hardships of his journey to Chartres in order to study the *Aphorisms* of Hippocrates of Cos; while from the twelfth century John of Salisbury, the leading northern humanist of the age, has left us an account of the masters which we shall later have occasion to cite. Nowhere else today can we drop back more easily into a cathedral city of the twelfth century, the peaceful town still dominated by its church and sharing, now as then,

> the minister's vast repose.
> Silent and gray as forest-leaguered cliff
> Left inland by the ocean's slow retreat,
> . . . . patiently remote
> From the great tides of life it breasted once,
> Hearing the noise of men as in a dream.

By the time the cathedral stood complete, with its "dedicated shapes of saints and kings," it had ceased to be an intellectual centre of the first importance, overshadowed by Paris fifty-odd miles away, so that Chartres never became a university.

The advantages of Paris were partly geographical,

partly political as the capital of the new French monarchy, but something must be set down to the influence of a great teacher in the person of Abelard. This brilliant young radical, with his persistent questioning and his scant respect for titled authority, drew students in large numbers wherever he taught, whether at Paris or in the wilderness. At Paris he was connected with the church of Mont-Sainte-Geneviève longer than with the cathedral school, but resort to Paris became a habit in his time, and in this way he had a significant influence on the rise of the university. In an institutional sense the university was a direct outgrowth of the school of Notre-Dame, whose chancellor alone had authority to license teaching in the diocese and thus kept his control over the granting of university degrees, which here as at Bologna were originally teachers' certificates. The early schools were within the cathedral precincts on the Ile de la Cité, that tangled quarter about Notre-Dame pictured by Victor Hugo which has long since been demolished. A little later we find masters and scholars living on the Little Bridge (Petit-Pont) which connected the island with the Left Bank of the Seine—this bridge gave its name to a whole school of philosophers, the Parvipontani—but by the thirteenth century they have overrun the Left Bank, thenceforth the Latin Quarter of Paris.

At what date Paris ceased to be a cathedral school and became a university, no one can say, though it was certainly before the end of the twelfth century. Universities, however, like to have precise dates to celebrate, and the University of Paris has chosen 1200, the year of its first royal charter. In that year, after certain students had been killed in a town and gown altercation, King Philip Augustus issued a formal privilege which punished his prévôt and recognized the exemption of the students and their servants from lay jurisdiction, thus creating that special position of students before the courts which has not yet wholly disappeared from the world's practice, though generally from its law. More specific was the first papal privilege, the bull *Parens scientiarum* of 1231,[8] issued after a two years' cessation of lectures growing out of a riot in which a band of students, having found "wine that was good and sweet to drink," beat up the tavern keeper and his friends till they in turn suffered from the prévôt and his men, a dissension in which the thirteenth century clearly saw the hand of the devil. Confirming the existing exemptions, the Pope goes on to regulate the discretion of the chancellor in conferring the license, at the same time that he recognizes the right of the masters and students "to make con-

[8] Trans. by L. Thorndike, *University Records and Life in the Middle Ages* (New York, 1944), pp. 35-39.

stitutions and ordinances regulating the manner and time of lectures and disputations, the costume to be worn," attendance at masters' funerals, the lectures of bachelors, necessarily more limited than those of fully fledged masters, the price of lodgings, and the coercion of members. Students must not carry arms, and only those who frequent the schools regularly are to enjoy the exemptions of students, the interpretation in practice being attendance at not less than two lectures a week.

While the word university does not appear in these documents, it is taken for granted. A university in the sense of an organized body of masters existed already in the twelfth century; by 1231 it had developed into a corporation, for Paris, in contrast to Bologna, was a university of masters. There were now four faculties, each under a dean: arts, canon law (civil law was forbidden at Paris after 1219), medicine, and theology. The masters of arts, much more numerous than the others, were grouped into four "nations": the French, including the Latin peoples; the Normans; the Picard, including also the Low Countries; and the English, comprising England, Germany, and the North and East of Europe. These four nations chose the head of the university, the rector, as he is still generally styled on the Continent, whose term, however, was short, being later only three months. If we may judge from such minutes as have survived, much of the time of the nations was devoted to consuming the fees collected from new members and new officers, or, as it was called, drinking up the surplus—at the Two Swords near the Petit-Pont, at the sign of Our Lady in the Rue S.-Jacques, at the Swan, the Falcon, the Arms of France, and scores of similar places. A learned monograph on the taverns of mediaeval Paris has been written from the records of the English nation alone. The artificial constitution of the nations seems to have encouraged rather than diminished the feuds and rivalries between the various regions represented at Paris, of which Jacques de Vitry has left a classic description: [4]

"They wrangled and disputed not merely about the various sects or about some discussions; but the differences between the countries also caused dissensions, hatreds, and virulent animosities among them, and they impudently uttered all kinds of affronts and insults against one another. They affirmed that the English were drunkards and had tails; the sons of France proud, effeminate, and carefully adorned like women. They said that the Germans were furious and obscene at their feasts; the Normans, vain and boastful; the

[4] As translated by D. C. Munro, *The Mediaeval Student* (University of Pennsylvania, Translations and Reprints; Philadelphia, 1899), p. 19 f.

Poitevins, traitors and always adventurers. The Burgundians they considered vulgar and stupid. The Bretons were reputed to be fickle and changeable, and were often reproached for the death of Arthur. The Lombards were called avaricious, vicious, and cowardly; the Romans, seditious, turbulent, and slanderous; the Sicilians, tyrannical and cruel; the inhabitants of Brabant, men of blood, incendiaries, brigands, and ravishers; the Flemish, fickle, prodigal, gluttonous, yielding as butter, and slothful. After such insults, from words they often came to blows."

Another university institution which goes back to twelfth-century Paris is the college. Originally merely an endowed hospice or hall of residence, the college early became an established unit of academic life at many universities. "The object of the earliest college-founders was simply to secure board and lodging for poor scholars who could not pay for it themselves"; [5] but in course of time the colleges became normal centres of life and teaching, absorbing into themselves much of the activity of the university. The colleges had buildings and endowments, if the university had not. There was a college at Paris as early as 1180; there were sixty-eight by 1500, and the system survived until the Revolution, to leave behind it only fragments of buildings or local names like the Sor-

[5] Rashdall, *op. cit.*, I, 500.

bonne of today, sole memento of that Collège de la Sorbonne founded for theologians by a confessor of St. Louis in the thirteenth century. Many other continental universities had their colleges, one of which, the ancient College of Spain at Bologna, still survives for the delectation of the few Spanish youths who reach its quiet courtyard. But of course the ultimate home of the college was Oxford and Cambridge, where it came to be the most characteristic feature of university life, arrogating to itself practically all teaching as well as direction of social life, until the university became merely an examining and degree-conferring body. Here the older colleges like Balliol, Merton, and Peterhouse date from the thirteenth century.

Paris was pre-eminent in the Middle Ages as a school of theology, and, as theology was the supreme subject of mediaeval study, "Madame la haute science" it was called, this means that it was pre-eminent as a university. "The Italians have the Papacy, the Germans have the Empire, and the French have Learning," ran the old saying; and the chosen abode of learning was Paris. Quite naturally Paris became the source and the model for northern universities. Oxford branched off from this parent stem late in the twelfth century, likewise with no definite date of foundation; Cambridge began somewhat later. The

German universities, none of them older than the fourteenth century, were confessed imitations of Paris. Thus the Elector Palatine, Ruprecht, in founding the University of Heidelberg in 1386—for these later universities were founded at specific dates—provides that it "shall be ruled, disposed, and regulated according to the modes and matters accustomed to be observed in the University of Paris, and that as a handmaid of Paris—a worthy one let us hope—it shall imitate the steps of Paris in every way possible, so that there shall be four faculties," four nations and a rector, exemptions for students and their servants, and even caps and gowns for the several faculties "as has been observed at Paris." [6]

By the end of the Middle Ages at least eighty universities had been founded in different parts of Europe.[7] Some of these were short-lived, many were of only local importance, others like Salerno flourished only to die, but some like Paris and Montpellier, Bologna and Padua, Oxford and Cambridge, Vienna and Prague and Leipzig, Coimbra and Salamanca, Cracow and Louvain, have an unbroken history of many centuries of distinction. And the great Euro-

[6] Translated in E. F. Henderson, *Select Historical Documents of the Middle Ages* (London and New York, 1892), pp. 262–266.

[7] Table in Rashdall, *op. cit.,* I, XXIV; map at beginning of Vol. II; and in Shepherd, *Historical Atlas* (New York, 1911), p. 100.

pean universities of more recent foundation, like Berlin, Strasbourg, Edinburgh, Manchester, and London, follow in their organization the ancient models. In America the earliest institutions of higher learning reproduced the type of the contemporary English college at a time when the university in England was eclipsed by its constituent colleges; but in the creation of universities in the later nineteenth century, America turned to the universities of the Continent and thus entered once more into the ancient inheritance. Even in the colonial period a sense of the general university tradition survived, for the charter of Rhode Island College in 1764 grants "the same privileges, dignities, and immunities enjoyed by the American colleges, and European universities."

What then is our inheritance from the oldest of universities? In the first place it is not buildings or a type of architecture, for the early universities had no buildings of their own, but on occasion used private halls and neighboring churches. After all, as late as 1775 the First Baptist Church in Providence was built "for the publick worship of Almighty God, and also for holding Commencement in"! Indeed one who seeks to reconstruct the life of ancient universities will find little aid in their existing remains. Salerno retains no monuments of its university, though its rare old cathedral, where Hildebrand lies buried, must have seen the passing of many generations of would-be physicians. In the halls and coats of arms of "many-domed Padua proud" we behold the Renaissance, not the Middle Ages. Even Bologna, *Bononia docta*, with its leaning towers and cool arcades, has no remains of university architecture earlier than the fourteenth century, from which date the oldest monuments of its professors of law gathered now into the municipal museum. Montpellier and Orleans preserve nothing from this period. Paris, too often careless of its storied past, can show today only the ancient church of Saint-Julien-le-Pauvre, where university meetings were often held, unless we count, as we should, the great cathedral in the Cité whence the university originally sprang. The oldest Cambridge college, Peterhouse, has only a fragment of its earliest buildings; the finest Cambridge monument, King's College chapel, is of the late fifteenth century. More than all others Oxford gives the deepest impression of continuity with an ancient past, Matthew Arnold's Oxford, "so venerable, so lovely . . . steeped in sentiment as she lies, spreading her gardens to the moonlight, and whispering from her towers the last enchantments of the Middle Age"; yet so far as the actual college buildings are concerned they have much more of sentiment than of the Middle Ages. Only at Merton which fixed the college type at Oxford, do any of the present structures carry us back of 1300, and nowhere is there much of the fourteenth century. Those venerable glories of Oxford, the Bodleian library, the tower of Magdalen, and the hall of Christ Church, belong to a much later age, the period of the Tudors, and thus by ordinary reckoning to modern times. When we say how very mediaeval, we often mean how very Tudor!

Neither does the continuity lie in academic form and ceremony, in spite of occasional survivals, like the conferring of degrees by the ring or the kiss of peace, or the timing of examinations by the hour glass as I have seen it at Portuguese Coimbra. Academic costume has in it some element of tradition where it is a daily dress as at Oxford, Cambridge, and Coimbra, but in America the tradition was broken by our ancestors, and the formal cap and gown current in the United States today are a product of modern Albany rather than of mediaeval Paris and Bologna. Even in their ancient homes the costumes have changed. "It is probable," says Rashdall,[8] "that no gown now worn in Oxford has much resemblance to its mediaeval ancestor." A student of mediaeval Padua would not recognize the variegated procession which wound through its streets last summer; Robert de Sorbon would rub his eyes at the non-mediaeval styles of the

[8] *Op. cit.*, III, 391 f.

gorgeous gowns which were massed on the stage of the great hall of the Sorbonne when President Wilson received his honorary degree in 1918.

It is, then, in institutions that the university tradition is most direct. First, the very name university, as an association of masters and scholars leading the common life of learning. Characteristic of the Middle Ages as such a corporation is, the individualistic modern world has found nothing to take its place. Next, the notion of a curriculum of study, definitely laid down as regards time and subjects, tested by an examination and leading to a degree, as well as many of the degrees themselves—bachelor, as a stage toward the mastership, master, doctor, in arts, law, medicine, and theology. Then the faculties, four or more, with their deans, and the higher officers such as chancellors and rectors, not to mention the college, wherever the residential college still survives. The essentials of university organization are clear and unmistakable, and they have been handed down in unbroken continuity. They have lasted more than seven hundred years—what form of government has lasted so long? Very likely all this is not final—nothing is in this world of flux—but it is singularly tough and persistent, suited to use and also to abuse, like Bryce's university with a faculty "consisting of Mrs. Johnson and myself," or the "eleven leading universities" of a certain state of the Middle West! Universities are at times criticised for their aloofness or their devotion to vocationalism, for being too easy or too severe, and drastic efforts have been made to reform them by abolishing entrance requirements or eliminating all that does not lead directly to bread and butter; but no substitute has been found for the university in its main business, the training of scholars and the maintenance of the tradition of learning and investigation. The glory of the mediaeval university, says Rashdall,[9] was "the consecration of Learning," and the glory and the vision have not yet perished from the earth. "The mediaeval university," it has been said, "was the school of the modern spirit." How the early universities performed this task will be the theme of the next lecture.

[9] *Op. cit.*, III, 442.

II

THE MEDIAEVAL PROFESSOR

IN THE last lecture we considered the mediaeval university as an institution. We come now to examine it as an intellectual centre. This involves some account of its course of study, its methods of teaching, and the status and freedom of its teachers. The element of continuity, so clear in institutions, is often less evident in the content of learning, but even here the thread is unbroken, the contrast with modern conditions less sharp than is often supposed.

The basis of education in the early Middle Ages consisted, as we have seen, of the so-called seven liberal arts. Three of these, grammar, rhetoric, and logic, were grouped as the trivium; the remaining four, arithmetic, geometry, astronomy, and music, made up the quadrivium. The first group was the more rudimentary, but the second was rudimentary enough. The number was fixed and the content standardized during the decadence of ancient learning, and the whole conception reached the Middle Ages chiefly in the book of a certain Martianus Capella, written in the early fifth century. These later ages of classical antiquity, in condensing and desiccating knowledge for their own more limited intelligence, were also unconsciously preparing for later times those small and convenient packages which alone could be carried as a *viaticum* through the stormy times of the Dark Ages. It was almost wholly as formulated in a few standard texts that the learning of the ancient world was transmitted to mediaeval times, and the authority of these manuals was so great that a list of those in use in any period affords an accurate index of the extent of its knowledge and the nature of its instruction. It was a bookish age, with great reverence for standard authorities, and its instruction followed closely the written word.

In the monastic and cathedral schools of the earlier period the text-books were few and simple, chiefly the Latin grammars of Donatus and Priscian with some elementary reading-books, the logical manuals of Boethius, as well as his arithmetic and music, a manual of rhetoric, the most elementary propositions of geometry, and an outline of practical astronomy

such as that of the Venerable Bede. Of Greek, of
course, there was none. This slender curriculum in
arts was much enlarged by the renaissance of the
twelfth century, which added to the store of western
knowledge the astronomy of Ptolemy, the complete
works of Euclid, and the Aristotelian logic, while at
the same time under the head of grammar great stimu-
lus was given to the study and reading of the Latin
classics. This classical revival, which is noteworthy
and comparatively little known, centred in such
cathedral schools as Chartres and Orleans, where the
spirit of a real humanism showed itself in an enthu-
siastic study of ancient authors and in the production
of Latin verse of a really remarkable quality. Certain
writings of one of these poets, Bishop Hildebert of Le
Mans, were even mistaken for "real antiques" by later
humanists. Nevertheless, though brilliant, this classical
movement was short-lived, crushed in its early youth
by the triumph of logic and the more practical studies
of law and rhetoric. In the later twelfth century John
of Salisbury inveighs against the logicians of his day,
with their superficial knowledge of literature; in the
university curriculum of the thirteenth century, literary studies have quite disappeared. Toward 1250,
when a French poet, Henri d'Andeli, wrote his *Battle
of the Seven Arts*, the classics are already the ancients,
fighting a losing battle against the moderns:

[29]

Logic has the students,
Whereas Grammar is reduced in numbers.

. . . .

Civil Law rode gorgeously
And Canon Law rode haughtily
Ahead of all the other arts.

If the absence of the ancient classics and of vernacular literature is a striking feature of the university curriculum in arts, an equally striking fact is the amount of emphasis placed on logic or dialectic. The earliest university statutes, those of Paris in 1215, require the whole of Aristotle's logical works, and throughout the Middle Ages these remain the backbone of the arts course, so that Chaucer can speak of the study of logic as synonymous with attendance at a university—

That un-to logik hadde longe y-go.

In a sense this is perfectly just, for logic was not only a major subject of study itself, it pervaded every other subject as a method and gave tone and character to the mediaeval mind. Syllogism, disputation, the orderly marshalling of arguments for and against specific theses, these became the intellectual habit of the age in law and medicine as well as in philosophy and theology. The logic, of course, was Aristotle's, and the other works of the philosopher soon followed, so that in the Paris course of 1254 we find also the *Ethics*, the *Metaphysics*, and the various treatises on natural science which had at first been forbidden to students. To Dante Aristotle had become "the Master of them that know," by virtue of the universality of his method no less than of his all-embracing learning. "The father of book knowledge and the grandfather of the commentator," no other writer appealed so strongly as Aristotle to the mediaeval reverence for the text-book and the mediaeval habit of formal thought. Doctrines like the eternity of matter which seemed dangerous to faith were explained away, and great and authoritative systems of theology were built up by the methods of the pagan philosopher. And all idea of literary form disappeared when everything depended on argument alone.

If the study of the classics became confined to examples and excerpts designed to illustrate the rules of grammar, rhetoric had a somewhat different fate by reason of its practical applications. The intellectual life of the Middle Ages was not characterized by spontaneous or widely diffused power of literary expression. Few were able to write, still fewer could compose a letter, and the professional scribes and notaries on whom devolved the greater part of the labor of mediaeval correspondence fastened upon the letter-writing of the period the stereotyped formalism of a conventional rhetoric. Regular instruction in the composition of letters and official acts was given in the schools and chanceries, and numerous professors, called *dictatores*, went about from place to place teaching this valuable art—"often and exceeding necessary for the clergy, for monks suitable, and for laymen honorable," as one rhetorician tells us. By the thirteenth century such masters had found a place in certain universities, especially in Italy and Southern France, and they advertised their wares in a way that has been compared to the claims of a modern business course—short and practical, with no time wasted on outgrown classical authors but everything fresh and snappy and up-to-date, ready to be applied the same day if need be! Thus one professor at Bologna derides the study of Cicero, whom he cannot recall having read, and promises to train his students in writing every sort of letter and official document which was demanded of the notaries and secretaries of his day. Since, as we shall see in the next lecture, such teachers specialized in the composition of student letters, chiefly skilful appeals to the parental purse, their practical utility was at once apparent. "Let us," says one writer, "take as our theme today that a poor and diligent student at Paris is to write his mother for necessary expenses." Would not every listener be sure that here at least he had found "the real thing"? The professor of rhetoric might also be called in to draft a university prospectus, like the circular issued in 1229 by the masters of the new University of Toulouse setting forth its superiority to Paris—theologians teaching in the pulpits and preaching at the street corners, lawyers magnifying Justinian and physicians Galen, professors of grammar and logic, and musicians with their organs, lectures on the books of natural philosophy then forbidden at Paris, low prices, a friendly populace, the way now prepared by the extirpation of the thorns of heresy, a land flowing with milk and honey, Bacchus reigning in the vineyards and Ceres in the fields under the mild climate desired by the philosophers of old, with plenary indulgence for all masters and students. Who could resist such an appeal from the South?

With grammar and rhetoric reduced to a subordinate position and the studies of the quadrivium receiving but scant attention, the arts course was mainly a course in logic and philosophy, plus so much of the natural sciences as could be apprehended by the scholastic study of the "natural books" of Aristotle. Laboratories there were none until long after the Middle Ages were past, and of history and the social sciences nothing was heard in universities until still later. Hard, close drill on a few well-thumbed books was the rule. The course in arts led normally to the master's degree in six years, with the baccalaureate somewhere on the way. Graduation in arts was the common preparation for professional study, being regularly required for theology and usual for intending lawyers and physicians. A sound tradition, to which the American world has given too little attention!

Contrary to a common impression, there were relatively few students of theology in mediaeval universities, for a prescribed theological training for the priesthood came in only with the Counter-Reformation. The requirements for admission were high; the course in theology itself was long; the books were costly. True, these books were commonly only the Bible and the *Sentences* of Peter Lombard, but the Bible in the Middle Ages might run into several volumes, especially when accompanied by gloss and commentary, and the copying of these by hand was a tedious and costly business. An ambitious student at Orleans who asks for money to buy a Bible and begin theology is advised by his father to turn rather to some lucrative profession. At the best, complain the Paris chancellors, students come late to theology, which should be the wife of their youth.

Medicine likewise was studied in books, chiefly Galen and Hippocrates with their Arabic translators and commentators, among whom Avicenna held the first place after the thirteenth century. Indeed Avicenna was still more firmly intrenched in the East, for as late as 1887 a majority of the native physicians in the Persian capital "knew no medicine but that of Avicenna." [1] Except for some advance in anatomy and surgery at certain southern schools, like Bologna and Montpellier, the mediaeval universities made no contributions to medical knowledge, for no subject was less adapted to their prevailing method of verbal and syllogistic dogmatism.

In law the basis of all instruction was inevitably the *Corpus Juris Civilis* of Justinian, for the customary law of mediaeval Europe was never a subject of university study. The central book was the *Digest*, summarizing the ripest fruits of Roman legal science, and it was their mastery of the *Digest* that gives preeminence to the mediaeval civilians. They brought the resources of the whole *Corpus* to bear on each passage in an elaborate gloss, and they showed refinement and subtlety of legal thought analogous to that of the scholastic philosophers. After all, "law is a form of scholasticism." But whereas the scholastic method in philosophy has lost hold on much of the modern world, the work of the glossators still survives. "In many respects," says Rashdall,[2] "the work of the School of Bologna represents the most brilliant

[1] E. G. Browne, *Arabian Medicine* (1921), p. 93.
[2] *Op. cit.*, I, 254–255.

achievement of the intellect of mediaeval Europe. The mediaeval mind had, indeed, a certain natural affinity for the study and development of an already existing body of Law. The limitations of its knowledge of the past and of the material Universe were not, to any appreciable extent, a bar to the mastery of a Science which concerns itself simply with the business and the relations of every-day life. The Jurist received his Justinian on authority as the Theologian received the Canonical and Patristic writings, or the Philosopher his Aristotle, while he had the advantage of receiving it in the original language. It had only to be understood, to be interpreted, developed, and applied. . . . The works of these men are, perhaps, the only productions of mediaeval learning to which the modern Professor of any science whatever may turn, not merely for the sake of their historical interest, not merely in the hope of finding ideas of a suggestive value, but with some possibility of finding a solution of the doubts, difficulties and problems which still beset the modern student."

The canon law was closely associated with the civil, indeed for many purposes it was desirable to graduate in both these subjects as a *Doctor utriusque juris*, or as we say a J.U.D. or an LL.D. Canon law was condemned by the theologians as a "lucrative" subject, which drew students away from pure learning toward the path of ecclesiastical preferment. By the thirteenth century the mediaeval church was a vast administrative machine which needed lawyers to run it, and a well-trained canonist had a good chance of rising to the highest dignities.[8] No wonder canon law attracted the ambitious, the wealthy, even the idle, for at Paris we are told that the lazy students frequented the lectures of the canonists in the middle of the morning, rather than the other courses which began at six. The standard text-book in canon law was the *Decretum* of Gratian, supplemented by the decretals of subsequent popes, especially the great collection which Gregory IX in 1234 distributed to the principal universities. The methods of studying these texts were the same as in the civil law, giving rise to the rich canonistic literature of the later Middle Ages and the marginal glosses for which, according to Dante, "the Gospel and the great doctors are deserted."

Of the text-books needed in all these subjects the university undertook to secure a supply at once sufficient, correct, and cheap, for the regulation of the book trade was one of the earliest and most valued of university privileges. As books were costly they were commonly rented, at a fixed price per quire, rather

[8] Sic heredes Gratiani
Student fieri decani,
Abbates, pontifices.

than owned; indeed the sale of books was hedged in by close restrictions designed to curb monopoly prices and to prevent their removal from town. The earliest Paris tariff, ca. 1286, lists for rent copies of one hundred and thirty-eight different books. In course of time many students came to have books of their own —a Bible, or at least some part of it, a piece of the *Digest*, perhaps even the "twenty bokes clad in blak or reed" of Chaucer's Oxford clerk. Whether rented or owned, the supply was not inconsiderable; on the Bolognese monuments each student has a book before him. So long as each copy had to be made by hand, accuracy was a matter of much importance, and the university had its supervisors and correctors who inspected periodically all the books for sale in the town. Moreover, at Bologna a constant supply of new books was secured by the requirement that every professor should turn over a copy of his repetitions and disputations to the stationers for publication. The principal books of law and theology were the natural outgrowth of university lectures. With demand and supply so largely concentrated in the universities, it is not surprising that these should have become the chief centres of the book trade and, as we should say, of the publishing business. So long as students could rent the books they required, there was less need for libraries than we might at first suppose, and it was quite natural that for long the university as such should have no library. In course of time, however, books were given for the use of students, chiefly in the form of bequests to the colleges, where they could be borrowed or consulted on the spot. By 1338 the oldest extant catalogue of the Sorbonne, the chief Paris library, lists 1722 volumes, many of them still to be seen in the Bibliothèque Nationale, while many an Oxford college still preserves codices which belonged to its library in the Middle Ages.

Turning from books to professors, we should note at the outset that the Middle Ages produced many excellent and renowned teachers. The mechanism of learning was still comparatively simple, its content not yet overwhelming, and, in spite of the close adherence to texts, there was a large scope for the personality of the instructor. Thus, long before the days of universities, Alcuin was the moving spirit in the revival of education at the court of Charlemagne and the monastery school of Tours, and two centuries later Gerbert of Rheims roused the wonder of contemporaries by his skilful use of the classics in the study of rhetoric and by devices for the teaching of astronomy so ingenious that they seemed in some way "divine." [4]

[4] Richer of Reims, *Histor.*, III, cc. 45-54; extracts translated in H. O. Taylor, *The Mediaeval Mind* (Cambridge, Mass., 1925), I, 289-293.

From the period of university origins we get a fairly clear impression of Abelard as a teacher and 'classroom entertainer,' bold, original, lucid, sharply polemical, always fresh and stimulating, and withal "able to move to laughter the minds of serious men." His procedure as exhibited in his *Sic et non* was to marshal authorities and arguments for and against specific propositions, a method which was soon imitated in Gratian's *Concord of Discordant Canons*, and, reenforced by the *New Logic* of Aristotle, was to culminate in the scholastic method of St. Thomas Aquinas and stamp itself upon the thought of many generations. Sharpening to the wits as this method was in the hands of Abelard and his successors, the very antagonism of yes or no as he formulated it left no room for intermediate positions, for those *nuances* of thought in which, as Renan pointed out, truth is usually to be found.

For a contemporary impression of the teachers of the twelfth century, nothing is so good as the oft-quoted passages in which John of Salisbury describes his *Wanderjahre* in France from 1136 to 1147, chiefly at Paris and Chartres.[5] Learning the rudiments of

[5] Translated in R. L. Poole, *Illustrations of the History of Mediaeval Thought,* 2nd ed. (London, 1920), pp. 203–212; A. O. Norton, *Readings in the History of Education* (Cambridge, Mass., 1909), pp. 28–34. What we know of these masters is

dialectic from Abelard, he continued under two other teachers of this art, one over-scrupulous in detail, perspicuous, brief, and to the point, the other subtle and profuse, showing that simple answers could not be given. "Afterward one of them went to Bologna and unlearned what he had taught, so that on his return he also untaught it." John then passed on to Chartres to study grammar under William of Conches and Bernard. The humane yet thorough teaching of literature here excited his warm admiration—close study, memorizing choice extracts, grammar taught by composition, imitation of excellent models but merciless exposure of borrowed finery, qualities which made Bernard "the most copious source of letters in Gaul in modern times." Returning to Paris after twelve years' absence, John found his old companions "as before, and where they were before; nor did they appear to have reached the goal in unravelling the old questions, nor had they added one jot of a proposition. The aims that once inspired them, inspired them still: they had progressed in one point only: they had unlearned moderation, they knew not modesty; in such wise that one might despair of their recovery. And thus experi-

___

analyzed by Poole, "The Masters of the Schools of Paris and Chartres in John of Salisbury's Time," *English Historical Review*, XXXV (1920), 321–342; reprinted in his *Studies in Chronology and History* (Oxford, 1934), pp. 223–247.

ence taught me a manifest conclusion, that, whereas dialectic furthers other studies, so if it remain by itself it lies bloodless and barren, nor does it quicken the soul to yield fruit of philosophy, except the same conceive from elsewhere."

The teachers of the thirteenth century who talk most about themselves are the professors of grammar and rhetoric like Buoncompagno at Bologna, John of Garlande at Paris, Ponce of Provence at Orleans, and Lorenzo of Aquileia at Naples and almost everywhere, but we shall make sufficient acquaintance with their inflated writings in other connections. More significant is the account which Odofredus gives of his lectures on the *Old Digest* at Bologna:

"Concerning the method of teaching the following order was kept by ancient and modern doctors and especially by my own master, which method I shall observe: First, I shall give you summaries of each title before I proceed to the text; second, I shall give you as clear and explicit a statement as I can of the purport of each law [included in the title]; third, I shall read the text with a view to correcting it; fourth, I shall briefly repeat the contents of the law; fifth, I shall solve apparent contradictions, adding any general principles of law [to be extracted from the passage], commonly called "Brocardica," and any distinctions or subtle and useful problems (*quaestiones*) arising out of the law with their solutions, as far as the Divine Providence shall enable me. And if any law shall seem deserving, by reason of its celebrity or difficulty, of a repetition, I shall reserve it for an evening repetition, for I shall dispute at least twice a year, once before Christmas and once before Easter, if you like.

"I shall always begin the *Old Digest* on or about the octave of Michaelmas [6 October] and finish it entirely, by God's help, with everything ordinary and extraordinary, about the middle of August. The *Code* I shall always begin about a fortnight after Michaelmas and by God's help complete it, with everything ordinary and extraordinary, about the first of August. Formerly the doctors did not lecture on the extraordinary portions; but with me all students can have profit, even the ignorant and the new-comers, for they will hear the whole book, nor will anything be omitted as was once the common practice here. For the ignorant can profit by the statement of the case and the exposition of the text, the more advanced can become more adept in the subtleties of questions and opposing opinions. And I shall read all the glosses, which was not the practice before my time." Then comes certain general advice as to the choice of teachers and the methods of study, followed by some general account of the *Digest*.

This course closed as follows: "Now gentlemen,

we have begun and finished and gone through this book as you know who have been in the class, for which we thank God and His Virgin Mother and all His saints. It is an ancient custom in this city that when a book is finished mass should be sung to the Holy Ghost, and it is a good custom and hence should be observed. But since it is the practice that doctors on finishing a book should say something of their plans, I will tell you something but not much. Next year I expect to give ordinary lectures well and lawfully as I always have, but no extraordinary lectures, for students are not good payers, wishing to learn but not to pay, as the saying is: All desire to know but none to pay the price. I have nothing more to say to you beyond dismissing you with God's blessing and begging you to attend the mass." [6]

Important as was the formal lecture in those days of few books and no laboratories, it was by no means the sole vehicle of instruction. A comprehensive survey of university teaching would need also to take account of the less formal "cursory" or "extraordinary" lectures, many of them given by mere bachelors; the

[6] Paris, Bibliothèque Nationale, MS. Lat. 4489, f. 102; F. C. von Savigny, *Geschichte des römischen Rechts im Mittelalter* (Heidelberg, 1834), III, 264, 541, 553; cf. Rashdall, *op. cit.*, I, 218; [according to a note in the revised edition, *ibid.*, p. 219 n.3, "this *Proemium* was in fact written by a pupil of Odofredus, Petrus Peregrossi, who taught at Orleans"].

reviews and "repetitions," which were often given in hospices or colleges in the evenings; and the disputations which prepared for the final ordeal of maintaining publicly the graduation thesis.

The class-rooms in which these lectures were given have long since disappeared. If the master's house had no suitable room, he literally hired a hall in some convenient neighborhood. At Paris such halls were mostly in a single street on the Left Bank, the Vicus Stramineus or Rue du Fouarre celebrated by Dante, apparently so-called from the straw-covered floor on which the students sat as they took notes. At Bologna the class-rooms were rather more ambitious. Here Buoncompagno, writing in 1235, has described an ideal lecture hall, quiet and clean, with a fair prospect from its windows, its walls painted green but with no pictures or statues to distract attention, the lecturer's seat elevated so that he may see and be seen by all, the seats of the students permanently assigned by nations and according to individual rank and fame; but he adds significantly, "I never had such a house myself and do not believe any of this sort was ever built." Our knowledge of the realities of the Bolognese class-room is derived chiefly from the monuments and miniatures of the professors of the fourteenth and fifteenth centuries, in which the master is regularly seated at a desk under a canopy on a raised platform, while the students have flat or inclined desks on which their books lie open. The professors, in medicine as in law, regularly have an open volume before them.

The nature of the final examination is best illustrated at Paris, where it is described in the *De conscientia* of that genial moralist, Robert de Sorbon, founder of the Sorbonne, by means of a suggestive parallel with the Last Judgment. Taking as his text Job's desire that his "adversary had written a book," and outlining his headings in the approved fashion of his time, Robert begins with the statement that if any one decides to seek the *licentia legendi* at Paris and cannot be excused from examination—as many of the great, by special favor, are—he would much like to be told by the chancellor, or by some one in his confidence, on what book he would be examined. Just as he would be a crazy student indeed, who, having found out which book this was, should neglect it and spend his time on others, even so is he mad who fails to study the book of his own conscience, in which we shall all, without exception, be examined at the great day. Moreover, if any one is rejected by the chancellor, he may be re-examined after a year, or it may be that, through the intercession of friends or by suitable gifts or services to the chancellor's relatives or other examiners, the chancellor can be induced to change his decision; whereas at the Last Judgment the sen-

tence will be final and there will be no help from
wealth or influence or stout assertion of ability as
canonist or civilian or of familiarity with all arguments and all fallacies. Then, if one fails before the
chancellor of Paris, the fact is known to but five or
six and the mortification passes away in time, while
the Great Chancellor, God, will refute the sinner "in
full university" before the whole world. The chancellor, too, does not flog the candidate, but in the Last
Judgment the guilty will be beaten with a rod of iron
from the valley of Jehosaphat through the length of
hell, nor can we reckon, like idle boys in the grammar-
schools, on escaping Saturday's punishment by feign-
ing illness, playing truant, or being stronger than the
master, or like them solace ourselves with the thought
that after all our fun is well worth a whipping. The
chancellor's examination, too, is voluntary; he does
not force any one to seek the degree, but waits as long
as the scholars wish, and is even burdened with their
insistent demands for examinations. In studying the
book of our conscience we should imitate the candi-
dates for the license, who eat and drink sparingly,
conning steadily the one book they are preparing,
searching out all the authorities that pertain to this,
and hearing only the professors that lecture on this
subject, so that they have difficulty in concealing from
their fellows the fact that they are preparing for

examination. Such preparation is not the work of five or ten days—though there are many who will not meditate a day or an hour on their sins—but of many years. At the examination the chancellor asks, "Brother, what do you say to this question, what do you say to this one and this one?" The chancellor is not satisfied with a verbal knowledge of books without an understanding of their sense, but unlike the Great Judge, who will hear the book of our conscience from beginning to end and suffer no mistakes, he requires only seven or eight passages in a book and passes the candidate if he answers three questions out of four. Still another difference lies in the fact that the chancellor does not always conduct the examination in person, so that the student who would be terrified in the presence of so much learning often answers well before the masters who act in the chancellor's place. Nothing is here said of the public maintenance of a thesis against all comers, an important final exercise which still survives as a form in German universities.

At Bologna there was first a "rigorous and tremendous examination" before doctors, each sworn to treat the candidate "as he would his own son." Then followed a public examination and inception which a letter home described as follows: " 'Sing unto the Lord a new song, praise him with stringed instruments

and organs, rejoice upon the high-sounding cymbals,'
for your son has held a glorious disputation, which
was attended by a great multitude of teachers and
scholars. He answered all questions without a mistake,
and no one could prevail against his arguments. Moreover he celebrated a famous banquet, at which both
rich and poor were honored as never before, and he
has duly begun to give lectures which are already so
popular that others' class-rooms are deserted and his
own are filled." The same rhetorician also tells of an
unsuccessful candidate who could do nothing in the
disputation but sat in his chair like a goat while the
spectators in derision called him rabbi; his guests at
the banquet had such eating that they had no will to
drink, and he must needs hire students to attend his
classes.

The social position of mediaeval professors must
be seen against the background of the social system of
a different age from ours. We come perhaps nearest
to modern conditions in the cities of Italy, where
there is evidence in the Middle Ages as now of the
distinguished position of many professors of medicine
and civil law. Many theologians and teachers of canon
law reached high places in the church such as bishop-
rics and cardinalates. Among the theologians and philosophers those of highest distinction were regularly
university professors: Thomas Aquinas, Albertus

Magnus, Bonaventura, all the great array of doctors angelic, invincible, irrefragable, seraphic, subtle, and universal. That these were also Dominicans or Franciscans withdrew them only partially from the world.

If, as some reformers maintain, the social position and self-respect of professors involve their management of university affairs, the Middle Ages were the great age of professorial control. The university itself was a society of masters when it was not a society of students. As there were no endowments of importance there were no boards of trustees, nor was there any such system of state control as exists on the Continent or in many parts of the United States. Administration in the modern sense was strikingly absent, but much time was consumed in various sorts of university meetings. In a quite remarkable degree the university was self-governing as well as self-respecting, escaping some of the abuses of a system which occasionally allows trustees or regents to speak of professors as their "hired men." Whether the individual professor was freer under such a system is another question, for the corporation of masters was apt to exercise a pretty close control over action if not over opinion, and the tyranny of colleagues is a form of that "tyranny of one's next-door neighbor" from which the world seems unable to escape.

There remains the question of the professor's intellectual liberty, the right to teach truth as he sees it, which we have come to call academic freedom. It is plain that much depends here, as with Pilate, on our conception of truth. If it is something to be discovered by search, the search must be free and untrammelled. If, however, truth is something which has already been revealed to us by authority, then it has only to be expounded, and the expositor must be faithful to the authoritative doctrine. Needless to say, the latter was the mediaeval conception of truth and its teaching. "Faith," it was held, "precedes science, fixes its boundaries, and prescribes its conditions." [7] "I believe in order that I may know, I do not know in order to believe," said Anselm. If reason has its bounds thus set, it befits reason to be humble. Let not the masters and students of Paris, says Gregory IX, "show themselves philosophers, but let them strive to become God's learned." The dangers of intellectual pride and reliance upon reason alone are illustrated by many characteristic stories of masters struck dumb in the midst of their boasting, like Étienne de Tournay, who, having proved the doctrine of the Trinity "so lucidly, so elegantly, so catholically," asserted that he could just as easily demolish his own proof. Mediaeval orthodoxy looked askance at mere cleverness, partly be-

[7] J. B. Alzog, *Manual of Universal Church History* (Cincinnati, 1876), II, 733.

cause much of the discussion of the schools led nowhere, partly because a mind that played too freely
about a proposition might easily fall into heresy. And
for the detection and punishment of heresy the mediaeval church organized a special system of courts
known as the Inquisition.

Such being the general conditions, what was the
actual situation? In practice freedom was general,
save in philosophy and theology. In law, in medicine,
in grammar and mathematics, men were normally free
to lecture and dispute as they would. As there was no
social problem in the modern sense and no teaching
of the social sciences as such, a fruitful source of difficulty was absent. So far as I know, no mediaeval professor was condemned for preaching free trade or free
silver or socialism or non-resistance. Moreover, while
individual treatises might be publicly burnt, as in the
later Roman Empire, there was no organized censor-
ship of books before the sixteenth century.

Now as to philosophy and theology. The trouble
lies of course with theology, for philosophy was free
save when it touched theological questions. But then,
philosophy is very apt to touch theological questions,
and all through the twelfth and thirteenth centuries
there was an intermittent fight between Christian theology and pagan philosophy as represented by the
works of Aristotle. It began with Abelard when he

[52]

tried to apply his logical method of inquiry to theology, and it went on when his contemporary, Gilbert de la Porrée, directed still more of the Aristotelian logic toward theological speculation. By the end of the twelfth century, the *New Logic* was pretty well assimilated, but then came Aristotle's *Metaphysics* and natural philosophy, with their Arabic commentators, the study of which at Paris was formally forbidden in 1210 and 1215. In 1231 the Pope requires them to be "examined and purged of all suspicion of error," but by 1254 they are a fixed part of the curriculum in arts, not expurgated but reconciled by interpretation to the Christian faith. A generation later there is a recrudescence of Averroism, emphasizing the doctrine of the eternity of matter and the determination of earthly acts by the heavenly bodies; and two hundred and nineteen errors of this party were condemned in 1277 by the bishop of Paris, who took occasion to lament incursions into theology on the part of students of arts. Throughout this period the whole of Aristotle was taught and studied at Paris, and his method was used by Thomas Aquinas to rear his vast structure of scholastic theology. Others reserved for themselves a wide range of philosophic speculation, and in case of trouble they could save themselves by falling back on the doctrine that what was true in philosophy might be false in theology, and *vice versa*.

With an eye to this question of freedom of teaching, I have gone through all the documents of the thirteenth century in the Paris *Chartularium*. Outside of the great controversies just mentioned the result is meagre. In 1241 a series of ten errors was examined and condemned by the chancellor and the professors of theology, a very abstract series of propositions dealing with the visibility of the divine essence, angels, and the exact abiding-place of glorified souls in the next world, whether in the empyrean or the crystalline heaven. In 1247 it appears that a certain Master Raymond had been imprisoned for his errors by the advice of the masters of theology, and one John de Brescain had been deprived of his right to teach because of certain errors in logic "which seemed to come near Arian heresy," thus confusing the subjects of the two faculties, whose bounds had been set by the fathers. In and about 1255 Paris was in a ferment over the so-called "Eternal Gospel," an apocalyptic treatise which foretold a new era of the Spirit, beginning in 1260, in which the New Testament, the Pope, and the hierarchy should be superseded. Accepted by certain advanced Franciscans, these doctrines became the occasion of a long conflict with the Mendicant orders, but with no very decisive results. In 1277 Paris received notice of thirty errors in arts condemned at Oxford, not as heretical but as sufficient to cause the deposition of the master teaching them; but when we find among them the abolition of the cases of Latin nouns and the personal endings of verbs (*ego currit, tu currit,* etc.), we are likely to sympathize more with their unfortunate students than with the deposed masters. One is reminded of the modern definition of academic freedom as "the right to say what one thinks without thinking what one says!"

With these as the only notable examples of interference with free teaching at the storm centre of theological speculation in the most active period of its history, we must infer that there was a large amount of actual freedom. Trouble arose almost entirely out of what was deemed theological heresy, or undue meddling with theological subjects by those who lacked theological training. Those who stuck to their job seem generally to have been let alone. As the great jurist Cujas replied in the sixteenth century when asked whether he was Protestant or Catholic, *Nihil hoc ad edictum praetoris.* Even within the more carefully guarded field of theology and philosophy, it is doubtful whether many found themselves cramped. Accepting the principle of authority as their starting-point, men did not feel its limitations as we should feel them now. A fence is no obstacle to those who do not desire to go outside, and many barriers that would seem intolerable to a more sceptical age were not felt as barriers by the schoolmen. He is free who feels himself free.

Furthermore, for those accustomed to the wide diversities of the modern world, it is easy to form a false impression of the uniformity and sameness of mediaeval thought. Scholasticism was not one thing but many, as its historians constantly remind us, and the contests between different schools and shades of opinion were as keen as among the Greeks or in our own day. And if the differences often seem minute or unreal to our distant eye, we can make them modern enough by turning, for example, to the old question of the nature of universal conceptions, which divided the Nominalists and Realists of the Middle Ages. Are universals mere names, or have they a real existence, independent of their individual embodiments? A bit arid it all sounds if we make it merely a matter of logic, but exciting enough as soon as it becomes a question of life. The essence of the Reformation lies implicit in whether we take a nominalist or a realist view of the church; the central problem of politics depends largely upon a nominalist or a realist view of the state. Upon the two sides of this last question millions of men have "all uncouthly died," all unconsciously too, no doubt, in the majority of cases, unaware of the ultimate issues of political authority for which they fought, but yet able to comprehend them when expressed in the concrete form of putting the interest of the state above the interest of its members.

In his own time and his own way the mediaeval professor often dealt with permanent human interests as he sharpened men's wits and kept alive the continuous tradition of learning.

III

THE MEDIAEVAL STUDENT

"A University," it has more than once been remarked by professors, "would be a very comfortable place were it not for the students." So far we have been considering universities from the point of view of professors; it is now the turn of the students, for whether these be regarded as a necessary evil or as the main reason for the university's existence, they certainly cannot be ignored. A mediaeval university was no regiment of colonels but "a society of masters *and scholars*," and to this second and more numerous element we must now direct our attention.

The mediaeval student is a more elusive figure than his teachers, for he is individually less conspicuous and must generally be seen in the mass. Moreover the mass is much diversified in time and space, so that generalization is difficult, what is true of one age and one university being quite untrue of other times and places. Even within the briefer span of American universities there are wide differences among the students of, let us say, Harvard in the seventeenth century, William and Mary in the eighteenth century, California in the nineteenth century, and Columbia in the twentieth century; and it would be impossible to make a true picture out of elements drawn indiscriminately from such disparate sources. Until the conditions at each university of the Middle Ages shall have been studied chronologically, no sound account of student life in general can be written, and this preliminary labor has nowhere been systematically attempted. At present we can do no more than indicate the principal sources of our information and the kind of light they throw upon student life.

Fortunately, out of the scattered remains of mediaeval times, there has come down to us a considerable body of material which deals, more or less directly, with student affairs. There are, for one thing, the records of the courts of law, which, amid the monotonous detail of petty disorders and oft-repeated offences, preserve now and then a vivid bit of mediaeval life—like the case of the Bolognese student who was attacked with a cutlass in a class-room, to the great damage and loss of those assembled to hear the lecture of a noble and egregious doctor of laws; or the student in 1289 who was set upon in the street in front of a lecture-room by a certain scribe, "who wounded him on the head with a stone, so that much blood gushed forth," while two companions gave aid and counsel, saying, "Give it to him, hit him," and when the offence had been committed ran away. So the coroners' rolls of Oxford record many a fatal issue of town and gown riots, while a recently published register of 1265 and 1266 shows the students of Bologna actively engaged in raising money by loans and by the sale of text-books. There are of course the university and college statutes, with their prohibitions and fines, regulating the subjects of conversation, the shape and color of caps and gowns, that academic dress which looks to us so mediaeval and is, especially in its American form, so very modern; careful also of the weightier matters of the law, like the enactment of New College against throwing stones in chapel, or the graded penalties at Leipzig for him who picks up a missile to throw at a professor, him who throws and misses, and him who accomplishes his fell purpose to the master's hurt. The chroniclers, too, sometimes interrupt their narrative of the affairs of kings and princes to tell of students and their doings, although their attention, like that of their modern successors, the newspapers, is apt to be caught by outbreaks of student lawlessness rather than by the wholesome routine of academic life.

Then we have the preachers of the time, many of them also professors, whose sermons contain frequent allusions to student customs; indeed if further evidence were needed to dispel the illusion that the mediaeval university was devoted to biblical study and religious nurture, the Paris preachers of the period would offer sufficient proof. "The student's heart is in the mire," says one of them, "fixed on prebends and things temporal and how to satisfy his desires." "They are so litigious and quarrelsome that there is no peace with them; wherever they go, be it Paris or Orleans, they disturb the country, their associates, even the whole university." Many of them go about the streets armed, attacking the citizens, breaking into houses, and abusing women. They quarrel among themselves over dogs, women, or what-not, slashing off one another's fingers with their swords, or, with only knives in their hands and nothing to protect their tonsured pates, rush into conflicts from which armed knights would hold back. Their compatriots come to their aid, and soon whole nations of students may be involved in the fray. These Paris preachers take us into the very atmosphere of the Latin Quarter and show us much of its varied activity. We hear the cries and songs of the streets—

Li tens s' en veit,
Et je n' ei riens fait;
Li tens revient,
Et je ne fais riens—

the students' tambourines and guitars, their "light and scurrilous words," their hisses and handclappings and loud shouts of applause at sermons and disputations. We watch them as they mock a neighbor for her false hair or stick out their tongues and make faces at the passers-by. We see the student studying by his window, talking over his future with his roommate, receiving visits from his parents, nursed by friends when he is ill, singing psalms at a student's funeral, or visiting a fellow-student and asking him to visit him—"I have been to see you, now come to our hospice."

All types are represented. There is the poor student, with no friend but St. Nicholas, seeking such charity as he can find or earning a pittance by carrying holy water or copying for others, in a fair but none too accurate hand, sometimes too poor to buy books or afford the expense of a course in theology, yet usually surpassing his more prosperous fellows who have an abundance of books at which they never look. There is the well-to-do student, who besides his books and desk will be sure to have a candle in his room and a comfortable bed with a soft mattress and luxurious coverings, and will be tempted to indulge the mediaeval fondness for fine raiment beyond the gown and hood and simple wardrobe prescribed by the statutes. Then there are the idle and aimless, drifting about from master to master and from school to school, and never hearing full courses or regular lectures. Some, who care only for the name of scholar and the income which they receive while attending the university, go to class but once or twice a week, choosing by preference the lectures on canon law, which leave them plenty of time for sleep in the morning. Many eat cakes when they ought to be at study, or go to sleep in the class-rooms, spending the rest of their time drinking in taverns or building castles in Spain (*castella in Hispania*); and when it is time to leave Paris, in order to make some show of learning such students get together huge volumes of calfskin, with wide margins and fine red bindings, and so with wise sack and empty mind they go back to their parents. "What knowledge is this," asks the preacher, "which thieves may steal, mice or moths eat up, fire or water destroy?" and he cites an instance where the student's horse fell into a river, carrying all his books with him. Some never go home, but continue to enjoy in idleness the fruits of their benefices. Even in vacation time, when the rich ride off with their servants and the poor trudge home under the burning sun, many idlers remain in Paris to their own and the city's harm. Mediaeval Paris, we should remember, was not only the incomparable "parent of the sciences," but also a place of good cheer and good fellowship and varied delights, a favorite resort not only of the studious but of country priests on a holiday; and it would not be strange if sometimes scholars prolonged their stay unduly and lamented their departure in phrases which are something more than rhetorical commonplace.

Then the student is not unknown to the poets of the period, among whom Rutebeuf gives a picture of thirteenth-century Paris not unlike that of the sermonizers, while in the preceding century Jean de Hauteville shows the misery of the poor and diligent scholar falling asleep over his books, and Nigel "Wireker" satirizes the English students at Paris in the person of an ass, Brunellus,—"Daun Burnell" in Chaucer—who studies there seven years without learning a word, braying at the end as at the beginning of his course, and leaving at last with the resolve to become a monk or a bishop. Best of all is Chaucer's incomparable portrait of the clerk of Oxenford, hollow, threadbare, unworldly—

> For him was lever have at his beddes heed
> Twenty bokes, clad in blak or reed,
> Of Aristotle and his philosophye,
> Than robes riche, or fithele, or gay sautrye.

. . . . . .

Souninge in moral vertu was his speche,
And gladly wolde he lerne, and gladly teche.

But after all, no one knows so much about student life as the students themselves, and it is particularly from what was written by and for them, the student literature of the Middle Ages, that I wish to draw more at length. Such remains of the academic past fall into three chief classes: student manuals, student letters, and student poetry. Let us consider them in this order.

The manuals of general advice and counsel addressed to the mediaeval scholar do not call for extended consideration. Formal treatises on the whole duty of students are characteristic of the didactic habit of mind of the Middle Ages, but the advice which they contain is apt to be of a very general sort, applicable to one age as well as another and lacking in those concrete illustrations which enliven the sermons of the period into useful sources for university life.

A more interesting type of student manual, the student dictionary, owes its existence to the position of Latin as the universal language of mediaeval education. Text-books were in Latin, lectures were in Latin, and, what is more, the use of Latin was compulsory in all forms of student intercourse. This rule may have been designed as a check on conversation, as well as an in-

centive to learning, but it was enforced by penalties
and informers (called wolves), and the freshman, or
yellow-beak as he was termed in mediaeval parlance,
might find himself but ill equipped for making himself understood in his new community. For his con-
venience a master in the University of Paris in the
thirteenth century, John of Garlande, prepared a
descriptive vocabulary, topically arranged and devoting a large amount of space to the objects to be seen in
the course of a walk through the streets of Paris. The
reader is conducted from quarter to quarter and from
trade to trade, from the book-stalls of the Parvis Notre-Dame and the fowl-market of the adjoining Rue
Neuve to the money-changers' tables and goldsmiths'
shops on the Grand-Pont and the bow-makers of the
Porte S.-Lazare, not omitting the classes of *ouvrières*
whose acquaintance the student was most likely to
make. Saddlers and glovers, furriers, cobblers, and
apothecaries, the clerk might have use for the wares of
all of them, as well as the desk and candle and writing-
materials which were the special tools of his calling;
but his most frequent relations were with the pur-
veyors of food and drink, whose agents plied their
trade vigorously through the streets and lanes of the
Latin Quarter and worked off their poorer goods on
scholars and their servants. There were the hawkers
of wine, crying their samples of different qualities

from the taverns; the fruit-sellers, deceiving clerks with lettuce and cress, cherries, pears, and green apples; and at night the vendors of light pastry, with their carefully covered baskets of wafers, waffles, and rissoles—a frequent stake at the games of dice among students, who had a custom of hanging from their windows the baskets gained by lucky throws of the six. The *pâtissiers* had also more substantial wares suited to the clerical taste, tarts filled with eggs and cheese and well-peppered pies of pork, chicken, and eels. To the *rôtissiers* scholars' servants resorted, not only for the pigeons, geese, and other fowl roasted on their spits, but also for uncooked beef, pork, and mutton, seasoned with garlic and other strong sauces. Such fare, however, was not for the poorer students, whose slender purses limited them to tripe and various kinds of sausage, over which a quarrel might easily arise and "the butchers be themselves butchered by angry scholars."

A dictionary of this sort easily passes into another type of treatise, the manual of conversation. This method of studying foreign langauges is old, as survivals from ancient Egypt testify, and it still spreads its snares for the unwary traveller who prepares to conquer Europe *à la* Ollendorff. To the writers of the later Middle Ages it seemed to offer an exceptional opportunity for combining Instruction in Latin with sound academic discipline, and from both school and university it left its monuments for our perusal. The most interesting of these handbooks is entitled a "Manual of Scholars who propose to attend universities of students and to profit therein," and while in its most common form it is designed for the students of Heidelberg about the year 1480, it could be adapted with slight changes to any of the German universities. "Rollo at Heidelberg," we might call it. Its eighteen chapters conduct the student from his matriculation to his degree, and inform him by the way on many subjects quite unnecessary for either. When the young man arrives he registers from Ulm; his parents are in moderate circumstances; he has come to study. He is then duly hazed after the German fashion, which treats the candidate as an unclean beast with horns and tusks which must be removed by officious fellow-students, who also hear his confession of sin and fix as the penance a good dinner for the crowd. He begins his studies by attending three lectures a day, and learns to champion nominalism against realism and the comedies of Terence against the law, and to discuss the advantages of various universities and the price of food and the quality of the beer in university towns. Then we find him and his room-mate quarrelling over a mislaid book; rushing at the first sound of the bell to dinner, where they debate the relative merits of veal and beans; or walking in the fields beyond the Neckar, perhaps by the famous Philosophers' Road which has charmed so many generations of Heidelberg youth, and exchanging Latin remarks on the birds and fish as they go. Then there are shorter dialogues: the scholar breaks the statutes; he borrows money, and gets it back; he falls in love and recovers; he goes to hear a fat Italian monk preach or to see the jugglers and the jousting in the market-place; he knows the dog-days are coming—he can feel them in his head! Finally our student is told by his parents that it is high time for him to take his degree and come home. At this he is much disturbed; he has gone to few lectures, and he will have to swear that he has attended regularly; he has not worked much and has incurred the enmity of many professors; his master discourages him from trying the examination; he fears the disgrace of failure. But his interlocutor reassures him by a pertinent quotation from Ovid and suggests that a judicious distribution of gifts may do much—a few florins will win him the favor of all. Let him write home for more money and give a great feast for his professors; if he treats them well, he need not fear the outcome. This advice throws a curious light upon the educational standards of the time; it appears to have been followed, for the manual closes with a set of forms inviting the masters to the banquet and the free bath by which it was preceded.

If university students had need of such elementary compends of morals and manners, there was obviously plenty of room for them in the lower schools as well, where they were apt to take the form of Latin couplets which could be readily impressed upon the pupil's memory. Such *statuta vel precepta scolarium* seem to have been especially popular in the later fifteenth century in those city schools of Germany whose importance has been so clearly brought out by recent historians of secondary education. Wandering often from town to town, like the roving scholars of an earlier age, these German boys had good need to observe the moral maxims thus purveyed. The beginning of wisdom was to remember God and obey the master, but the student had also to watch his behavior in church and lift up his voice in the choir—compulsory attendance at church and singing in the choir being a regular feature of these schools—keep his books clean, and pay his school bills promptly. Face and hands should be washed in the morning, but the baths should not be visited without permission, nor should boys run on the ice or throw snowballs. Sunday was the day for play, but this could be only in the churchyard, where boys must be careful not to play

with dice or break stones from the wall or throw anything over the church. And whether at play or at
home, Latin should always be spoken.

More systematic is a manual of the fifteenth century
preserved in a manuscript of the Bibliothèque Nationale at Paris.[1] "Since by reason of imbecility youths
cannot advance to a knowledge of the Latin tongue
by theory alone," the author has for their assistance
prepared a set of forms which contain the expressions
most frequently employed by clerks. Beginning with
the courtesies of school life, for obedience and due
reverence for the master are the beginning of wisdom,
the boy learns how to greet his master and to take
leave, how to excuse himself for wrong-doing, how
to invite the master to dine or sup with his parents—
there are half a dozen forms for this! He is also taught
how to give proper answers to those who seek to test
his knowledge, "that he may not appear an idiot in the
sight of his parents." "If the master asks, 'Where
have you been so long?' " he must be ready, not only
to plead the inevitable headache or failure to wake up,
but also to express the causes of delay well known to
any village boy. He had to look after the house or feed
the cattle or water the horse; he was detained by a
wedding, by picking grapes, or making out bills, or
—for these were German boys—by helping with

[1] MS. Lat. n. a. 619, ff. 28–35.

the brew, fetching beer, or serving drink to guests.

In school after the "spiritual refection" of the morning singing-lesson comes refection of the body, which is placed after study hours because "the imaginative virtue is generally impeded in those who are freshly sated." In their talk at luncheon or on the playground "clerks are apt to fall from the Latin idiom into the mother tongue," and for him who speaks German the discretion of the master has invented a dunce's symbol called an ass, which the holder tries hard to pass on to another. "Wer wel ein Griffel kouffe[n]?" "Ich wel ein Griffel kouffen." "Tecum sit asinus." "Ach, quam falsus es tu!" Sometimes the victim offers to meet his deceiver after vespers, with the usual schoolboy brag on both sides. As it is forbidden to come to blows in school, the boys are taught to work off their enmities and formulate their complaints in Latin dialogue. "You were outside the town after dark. You played with laymen Sunday. You went swimming Monday. You stayed away from matins. You slept through mass." "Reverend master, he has soiled my book, he shouts after me wherever I go, he calls me names." Besides the formal disputations the scholars discuss such current events as a street fight, a cousin's wedding, the coming war with the duke of Saxony, or the means of getting to Erfurt, whither one of them is going when he is sixteen to study at the university.

The great ordeal of the day was the master's quiz on Latin grammar, when every one was questioned in turn (*auditio circuli*). The pupils rehearse their declensions and conjugations and the idle begin to tremble as the hour draws near. There is some hope that the master may not come. "He has guests." "But they will leave in time." "He may go to the baths." "But it is not yet a whole week since he was there last." "There he comes. Name the wolf, and he forthwith appears." Finally the shaky scholar falls back on his only hope, a place near one who promises to prompt him.

"When the recitation is over and the lesson given out, rejoicing begins among the youth at the approach of the hour for going home," and they indulge in much idle talk "which is here omitted, lest it furnish the means of offending." Joy is, however, tempered by the contest which precedes dismissal, "a serious and furious disputation for the *palmiterium*," until one secures the prize and another has the *asinus* to keep till next day.

After school the boys go to play in the churchyard, the sports mentioned being hoops, marbles (apparently), ball (during Lent), and a kind of counting game. The author distinguishes hoops for throwing and for rolling, spheres of wood and of stone, but the subject soon becomes too deep for his Latin, and in the midst of this topic the treatise comes to an abrupt conclusion.

In some of its forms the student manual touches on territory already occupied by another type of mediaeval handbook, the manual of manners, which under such titles as "The Book of Urbanity," "The Courtesies of the Table," etc., enjoyed much popularity from the thirteenth century onward. Such manuals have, however, none of the polish of Castiglione's *Courtier* or the elaborateness of the modern book of etiquette. Those who have not mastered the use of knife and fork have little use for the finer points of social intercourse, and the readers of the mediaeval manuals were still at the a b c's in the matter of behavior. Wash your hands in the morning and, if you have time, your face; use your napkin and handkerchief; eat with three fingers, and don't gorge; don't be boisterous or quarrelsome at table; don't stare at your neighbor or his plate; don't criticise the food; don't pick your teeth with your knife—such, with others still more elementary, are the maxims which meet us in this period, in Latin and French, in English, German, and Italian, but regularly in verse. Now and then there is a further touch of the age: scrape bones with your knife but don't knaw them; when you have done with them, put them in a bowl or on the floor!

If the correspondence of mediaeval students were preserved for us in casual and unaffected detail, nothing could give a more vivid picture of university conditions. Unfortunately in some respects for us, the Middle Ages were a period of forms and types in letter-writing as in other things; and for most men the writing of a letter was less an expression of individual feeling and experience than it was the laborious copying of a letter of some one else, altered where necessary to suit the new conditions. And if something fresh or individual was produced, there was small chance of preserving it, since it was on that account all the less likely to be useful to a future letter-writer—"so careful of the type, so careless of the single" letter, history seems. The result is that the hundreds of student letters which have reached us in the manuscripts of the Middle Ages have come down through the medium of collections of forms or complete letter-writers, shorn of most of their individuality but for that very reason reflecting the more faithfully the fundamental and universal phases of university life.

By far the largest element in the correspondence of mediaeval students consists of requests for money; "a student's first song is a demand for money," says a weary father in an Italian letter-writer, "and there will never be a letter which does not ask for cash." How to secure this fundamental necessity of student life was doubtless one of the most important problems that confronted the mediaeval scholar, and many were the models which the rhetoricians placed before him in proof of the practical advantages of their art. The letters are generally addressed to parents, sometimes to brothers, uncles, or ecclesiastical patrons; a much copied exercise contained twenty-two different methods of approaching an archdeacon on this ever-delicate subject. Commonly the student announces that he is at such and such a centre of learning, well and happy but in desperate need of money for books and other necessary expenses. Here is a specimen from Oxford, somewhat more individual than the average and written in uncommonly bad Latin:

"B. to his venerable master A., greeting. This is to inform you that I am studying at Oxford with the greatest diligence, but the matter of money stands greatly in the way of my promotion, as it is now two months since I spent the last of what you sent me. The city is expensive and makes many demands; I have to rent lodgings, buy necessaries, and provide for many other things which I cannot now specify. Wherefore I respectfully beg your paternity that by the promptings of divine pity you may assist me, so that I may be able to complete what I have well begun. For you must know that without Ceres and Bacchus Apollo grows cold."

If the father was close-fisted, there were special reasons to be urged: the town was dear—as university towns always are!—the price of living was exceptionally high owing to a hard winter, a siege, a failure of crops, or an unusual number of scholars; the last messenger had been robbed or had absconded with the money; the son could borrow no more of his fellows or of the Jews; and so on. The student's woes are depicted in moving language, with many appeals to paternal vanity and affection. At Bologna we hear of the terrible mud through which the youth must beg his way from door to door, crying, "O good masters," and coming home empty-handed. In an Austrian formulary a scholar writes from the lowest depths of prison, where the bread is hard and moldy, the drink water mixed with tears, the darkness so dense that it can actually be felt. Another lies on straw with no covering, goes without shoes or shirt, and eats he will not say what—a tale designed to be addressed to a sister and to bring in response a hundred *sous tournois*, two pairs of sheets, an l ten ells of fine cloth, all sent without her husband's knowledge. "We have made little glosses, we owe money," is the terse summary of two students at Chartres.

To such requests the proper answer was, of course, an affectionate letter, commending the young man's industry and studious habits and remitting the desired amount. Sometimes the student is cautioned to moderate his expenses—he might have got on longer with what he had, he should remember the needs of his sisters, he ought to be supporting his parents instead of trying to extort money from them, etc. One father —who quotes Horace!—excuses himself because of the failure of his vineyards. It often happened, too, that the father or uncle has heard bad reports of the student, who must then be prepared to deny indignantly all such aspersions as the unfounded fabrications of his enemies. Here is an example of paternal reproof taken from an interesting collection relating to Franche-Comté:

"To his son G. residing at Orleans P. of Besançon sends greetings with paternal zeal. It is written, 'He also that is slothful in his work is brother to him that is a great waster.' I have recently discovered that you live dissolutely and slothfully, preferring license to restraint and play to work and strumming a guitar while the others are at their studies, whence it happens that you have read but one volume of law while your more industrious companions have read several. Wherefore I have decided to exhort you herewith to repent utterly of your dissolute and careless ways, that you may no longer be called a waster and your shame may be turned to good repute."

In the models of Ponce de Provence we find a teacher writing to a student's father that while the young man is doing well in his studies, he is just a trifle wild and would be helped by judicious admonition. Naturally the master does not wish it known that the information came through him, so the father writes his son:

"I have learned—not from your master, although he ought not to hide such things from me, but from a certain trustworthy source—that you do not study in your room or act in the schools as a good student should, but play and wander about, disobedient to your master and indulging in sport and in certain other dishonorable practices which I do not now care to explain by letter." Then follow the customary exhortations to reform.

Two boys at Orleans thus describe their arrival at this centre of learning:

"To their dear and respected parents M. Martre, knight, and M. his wife, M. and S. their sons send greeting and filial obedience. This is to inform you that, by divine mercy, we are living in good health in the city of Orleans and are devoting ourselves wholly to study, mindful of the words of Cato, 'To know anything is praiseworthy.' We occupy a good dwelling, next door but one to the schools and market-place, so that we can go to school every day without wetting our feet. We have also good companions in the house with us, well advanced in their studies and of excellent habits—an advantage which we well appreciate, for as the Psalmist says, 'With an upright man thou wilst show thyself upright.' "

Such youths were slow to quit academic life. Again and again they ask permission to have their term of study extended; war might break out, parents or brothers die, an inheritance have to be divided, but the student pleads always for delay. He desires to "serve longer in the camp of Pallas"; in any event he cannot leave before Easter, as his masters have just begun important courses of lectures. A scholar is called home from Siena to marry a lady of many attractions; he answers that he deems it foolish to desert the cause of learning for the sake of a woman, "for one may always get a wife, but science once lost can never be recovered."

The time to leave, however, must come at last, and then the great problem is money for the expenses of commencement, or, as it was then called, inception. Thus a student at Paris asks a friend to explain to his father, "since the simplicity of the lay mind does not understand such things," how at length after much study nothing but lack of money for the inception banquet stands in the way of his graduation. From Orleans D. Boterel writes to his dear relatives at Tours that he is laboring over his last volume of law and on its completion will be able to pass to his licentiate provided they send him a hundred *livres* for the necessary expenses. An account of the inception at Bologna was quoted in the preceding chapter.[2]

Unlike the student letters, which range over the whole of the later Middle Ages, mediaeval student poetry, or rather the best of it, is limited to a comparatively short period comprised roughly within the years 1125 and 1225, and is closely connected with the classical phase of the twelfth-century renaissance. It is largely the work of the wandering clerks of the period—students, ex-students, professors even—moving from town to town in search of learning and still more of adventure, nominally clerks but leading often very unclerical lives. "Far from their homes," says Symonds, "without responsibilities, light of purse and light of heart, careless and pleasure-seeking, they ran a free, disreputable course." "They are wont," writes a monk of the twelfth century, "to roam about the world and visit all its cities, till much learning makes them mad; for in Paris they seek liberal arts, in Orleans classics, at Salerno medicine, at Toledo magic,

[2] Supra, p. 48 f.

but nowhere manners and morals." Their chief hab-
itat, however, was nothern France, the center of the
new literary renaissance.

Possibly from some obscure allusion to Goliath the
Philistine, these wandering clerks took the name Goliardi and their verse is generally known as Goliardic
poetry. This literature is for the most part anony-
mous, though recent research has individualized certain writers of the group, notably a Master Hugh,
canon of Orleans, ca. 1142, styled the Primate, and
the so-called Archpoet. The Primate, mordant, dia-
bolically clever, thoroughly disreputable, became famous for generations as "an admirable improviser,
who if he had but turned his heart to the love of God
would have had a great place in divine letters and have
proved most useful to God's church." The Archpoet
is found chiefly in Italy from 1161 to 1165, going
"on his own" in spring and summer but when autumn
comes on turning to beg shirt and cloak from his pa-
tron, the archbishop of Cologne. Ordered to compose
an epic for the emperor in a week, he replies he cannot write on an empty stomach—the quality of his
verse depends on the quality of his wine:

Tales versus facio quale vinum bibo.

Good wine he must at times have found, for he composed the masterpiece of the whole school, the Con-

fession of a Goliard, that unforgettable description of the burning temptations of Pavia which contains the famous glorification of the joys of the tavern:

> In the public house to die
>   Is my resolution;
> Let wine to my lips be nigh
>   At life's dissolution;
> That will make the angels cry,
>   With glad elocution,
> "Grant this toper, God on high,
>   Grace and absolution!"

Though written in Latin, the Goliardic verse has abandoned the ancient metrical system for the rhyme and accent of modern poetry, but even the best of modern versions, such as those of John Addington Symonds, from which I am quoting, fail to render the swing, the lilt, the rhythmical flow of the original. Its authors are familiar with classical mythology and especially with the writings of Ovid, whose precepts, copied even in severe Cluny, were freely followed. Most of all is this poetry classical in its frankly pagan view of life. Its gods are Venus and Bacchus, also Decius, the god of dice. Love and wine and spring, life on the open road and under the blue sky, these are the common subjects; the spirit is that of an intense delight in the world that is, a joy in mere living, such as one finds in the Greek and Roman poets or in that sonorous song of a later age which the academic world still cherishes,

Gaudeamus igitur iuvenes dum sumus.

In general the Goliardic poetry is of an impersonal sort giving us few details from any particular place, but reflecting the gayer, more jovial, less reputable side of the life of mediaeval clerks. The worshipful order of vagrants is described, open to men of every condition and every clime, with its rules which are no rules, late-risers, gamesters, roysterers, proud that none of its members has more than one coat to his back, begging their way from town to town with requests for money which sound like students' letters in verse:

> I, a wandering scholar lad,
>   Born for toil and sadness,
> Oftentimes am driven by
>   Poverty to madness.
>
> Literature and knowledge I
>   Fain would still be earning,
> Were it not that want of pelf
>   Makes me cease from learning.
>
> These torn clothes that cover me
>   Are too thin and rotten;

Oft I have to suffer cold,
  By the warmth forgotten.

Scarce I can attend at church,
  Sing God's praises duly;
Mass and vespers both I miss,
  Though I love them truly.

Oh, thou pride of N——,
  By thy worth I pray thee
Give the suppliant help in need,
  Heaven will sure repay thee.

Take a mind unto thee now
  Like unto St. Martin;
Clothe the pilgrim's nakedness,
  Wish him well at parting.

So may God translate your soul
  Into peace eternal,
And the bliss of saints be yours
  In His realm supernal.

The brethren greet each other at wayside taverns with songs like this:

We in our wandering,
Blithesome and squandering,
  Tara, tantara, teino!

Eat to satiety,
Drink with propriety;
   Tara, tantara, teino!

Laugh till our sides we split,
Rags on our hides we fit;
   Tara, tantara, teino!

Jesting eternally,
Quaffing infernally:
   Tara, tantara, teino!
                  etc.

The assembled topers are described in another poem:

Some are gaming, some are drinking,
Some are living without thinking;
And of those who make the racket,
Some are stripped of coat and jacket;
Some get clothes of finer feather,
Some are cleaned out altogether;
No one there dreads death's invasion,
But all drink in emulation.

Then they sacrilegiously drink once for all prisoners
and captives, three times for the living, a fourth time
for the whole body of Christians, a fifth for those de-
parted in the faith, and so on to the thirteenth for
those who travel by land or water, and a final and un-

limited potation for king and Pope. Such poetry is plainly the expression of a "wet" age.

Often bibulous and erotic, the Goliardic verse contains a large amount of parody and satire. Appealing to a public familiar with scripture and liturgy, its authors parody anything—the Bible, hymns to the Virgin, the canon of the mass, as in the "Drinkers' Mass" and the "Office for Gamblers." One of the best-known pieces is a satire on the Papacy under the caption of "The Gospel according to Mark-s of silver." This is only one of many bitter attacks on Rome, while the pride, hardness, and greed of the higher clergy are portrayed in "Golias the Bishop." The point of view in general is that of the lower clergy, especially the looser, wandering, undisciplined element which frequented the schools and the roads, the *jongleurs* of the clerical world, familiar subjects of ecclesiastical legislation since the ninth century.

Poetry of this sort is so contrary to conventional conceptions of the Middle Ages that some writers have denied its mediaeval character. "It is," says one, "mediaeval only in the chronological sense," while others find in it close affinities with the spirit of the Renaissance or of the Reformation. It would be more consonant with the spirit of history to enlarge our ideas of the Middle Ages so as to correspond to the facts of mediaeval life. The Goliardi were neither humanists before the Renaissance nor reformers before the Reformation; they were simply men of the Middle Ages who wrote for their own time. If the writings of these northern and chiefly French clerks seem to anticipate the Italian Renaissance, it may be that the Renaissance began earlier and was less specifically Italian than has been supposed. If the authors are more secular, even more earthy, than we should expect clerks to be, we must learn to expect something different. In lyric poetry, as in the epic and the drama, we are now learning more of the close interpenetration of the lay and ecclesiastical worlds, no longer separated by the air-tight partitions which the imagination of a later day interposed. And whether their spirit was lay or ecclesiastical, the Goliardi were certainly human; they saw and felt life keenly, and they wrote of what they knew.

It is time to redress the balance with a word about a less obtrusive element, the good student. "The life of the virtuous student," says Hastings Rashdall, "has no annals," [3] and in all ages he has been less conspicuous than his more dashing fellows. Thus the ideal scholar of the sermons is a bit colorless but obedient, respectful, eager to learn, assiduous at lectures, and bold in debate, pondering his lessons even during his

[3] *Op cit.*, III, 441.

evening promenades by the river. The ideal student of the manuals is he who practices their precepts. The typical student of the letters has already described himself as devoted wholly to study, though somewhat short of money. The good student of the poems—there is no such person! Student poetry was "not all bacchic or erotic or profane," [4] but much of it was, and we must not look here for the more serious side of academic life. Jean de Hauteville's account of the poor and industrious scholar is representative of a large class of students but not of a large body of poetry. The good student's occupations are best reflected in the course of study, his assiduity best seen in his note-books and disputations. The documents which concern the educational side of the university are also a source for student life! It has been observed that the alumni reunions of our own day are often more prolific in recollections of student escapades than of the daily performance of the allotted task. The studious lad of today never breaks into the headlines as such, and no one has seen fit to produce a play or a film "featuring the good student." Yet everyone familiar with contemporary universities knows that the serious student exists in large numbers, and it has been shown conclusively that the distinction he there achieves reflects itself in his later life. So it was in the Middle

[4] *Op. cit.*, III, 435, n. 4.

Ages. The law students of Bologna insisted on their money's worth of teaching from their professors. The examinations described by Robert de Sorbon required serious preparation. Not only was the vocational motive a strong incentive to study in the mediaeval university, but there was much enthusiasm for knowledge and much discussion of intellectual subjects. The greater universities, at least, were intellectually very much alive, with something of that "religion of learning" which had earlier called Abelard's pupils into the wilderness, there to build themselves huts that they might feed upon his words. The books of the age were in large measure written by its professors, and the students had the advantage of seeing them in the making and thus drinking of learning at its fountainhead. Then as now, the moral quality of a university depended on the intensity and seriousness of its intellectual life.

If we consider the body of student literature as a whole, its most striking, and its most disappointing, characteristic is its lack of individuality. The *Manuale Scholarium* is written for the use of all scholars who propose to attend universitities of students. The letters are made as general as possible in order to fit the need of any student who wants money, clothes, or books. Even the poems, where we have some right to expect personal expression of feeling, have the generic character of most mediaeval poetry; they are for the most part the voice of a class, not of individuals.

At the same time it must be remembered that this characteristic of the student productions, if it robs them of something of their interest, increases their historical value. The historian deals with the general rather than the particular, and his knowledge must be built up by a painful collection and comparison of individual facts, which are often too few or to unlike to admit of sound generalization. In the case of these student records, however, that labor has already been performed for him; in the form in which they come down to us they have lost, at the hands of the students themselves, what is local and peculiar and exceptional, and have become, what in view of the nature of our information no historian could hope to make them, the generalized experience of centuries of student life.

It is this broadly human quality that gives the productions of the mediaeval student a special interest for the world of today. In substance, though not in form, many of them are almost as representative of modern Harvard or Yale as of mediaeval Oxford or Paris. The Latin dialogue and disputation, the mud of Bologna, and the money-changers of the Grand-Pont, belong plainly in the Middle Ages and not in our time; but money and clothing, rooms, teachers, and books, good cheer and good fellowship, have been subjects of interest at all times and all places. A professor of history once said that the greatest difficulty of historical teaching lay in convincing pupils that the events of the past did not all happen in the moon. The Middle Ages are very far away, farther from us in some respects than is classical antiquity, and it is very hard to realize that men and women, then and now, are after all much the same human beings. We need constantly to be reminded that the fundamental factors in man's development remain much the same from age to age and must so remain as long as human nature and physical environment continue what they have been. In his relations to life and learning the mediaeval student resembled his modern successor far more than is often supposed. If his environment was different, his problems were much the same; if his morals were perhaps worse, his ambition was as active, his rivalries as intense, his desire for learning quite as keen. And for him as for us, intellectual achievement meant membership in that city of letters not made with hands, "the ancient and universal company of scholars."

BIBLIOGRAPHICAL NOTE

[It seemed advisable to keep all the titles of books and articles listed in the bibliographical note of the original edition of 1923 in order to show from what sources C. H. Haskins drew his account. The editor has indicated, in square brackets, later or revised editions of works mentioned by Haskins, and he has also supplemented the bibliography on the most important topics discussed by Haskins with some of the essential books or articles published since 1923. In a few instances, bibliographical data have been made more complete or have been corrected, and these changes have not been indicated in brackets.—T. E. Mommsen.]

I

[General bibliography: G. C. Boyce, "American Studies in Medieval Education," *Progress of Medieval and Renaissance Studies*, XIX (1947), 6–30.]

The standard work on mediaeval universities is Hastings Rashdall, *The Universities of Europe in the Middle*

Ages (Oxford, 1895), to which my indebtedness will be apparent throughout; [a revised edition of Rashdall's still absolutely indispensable work was edited by F. M. Powicke and A. B. Emden, 3 vols. (Oxford, 1936)].

[See also S. D'Irsay, *Histoire des universités françaises et étrangères*, vol. I: *Moyen Age et Renaissance* (Paris, 1933); N. Schachner, *The Mediaeval Universities* (New York, 1938). For literature prior to 1929, consult the revised edition of L. J. Paetow, *A Guide to the Study of Medieval History* (New York, 1931)].

Important materials are conveniently accessible in translation in D. C. Munro, *The Mediaeval Student* (University of Pennsylvania, Translations and Reprints, vol. II, no. 3; Philadelphia, 1899); and A. O. Norton, *Readings in the History of Education: Mediaeval Universities* (Cambridge, Mass., 1909); [the most valuable collection of primary materials on the universities now available in translations is that by L. Thorndike, *University Records and Life in the Middle Ages* (New York, 1944)].

Bologna now has a *Chartularium Studii Bononiensis; Documenti per la storia della Università di Bologna dalle origini fino al secolo XV* (since 1907), and a special series of *Studi e Memorie per la storia della Università di Bologna* (since 1907); [see also the series *Universitatis Bononiensis Monumenta* (since 1932)]. The municipal history of the period has been studied by A. Hessel, *Geschichte der Stadt Bologna von 1116 bis 1280* (Berlin, 1910). [The newest histories of the university are those by A. Sorbelli, *Storia della Università di Bologna: Il medioevo* (Bologna, 1940), and C. Calcaterra, *Alma mater studiorum: L'Università di Bologna nella storia della cultura e della civiltà* (Bologna, 1948)].

Light has recently been thrown on Salerno by the studies of Giacosa and Sudhoff and the dissertations of Sudhoff's pupils; [see also P. O. Kristeller, "The School of Salerno: Its development and its contribution to the history of learning," *Bulletin of the History of Medicine*, XVII (1945), 138–194]; its most important product, *The School of Salernum*, can be read in the quaint Elizabethan version of Sir John Harrington, reprinted (London, 1922) with a good note by F. H. Garrison and a less valuable preface by Francis R. Packard.

Paris still lacks a modern historian. [Compare the very useful bibliography on the university and colleges of Paris which has been compiled by A. L. Gabriel, *Student Life in Ave Maria College, Mediaeval Paris: History and Chartulary of the College* (Notre Dame, Ind., 1955); general introductions have been presented by J. Bonnerot, *La Sorbonne: Sa vie, son rôle, son oeuvre à travers les siècles* (Paris, 1927), and by the articles of L. Halphen, P. Glorieux, G. Dupont-Ferrier, G. Le Bras and C. Samaran in the collection *Aspects de l'Université de Paris*, ed. by J. Calvet (Paris, 1949); on the institution of the "nations" in Paris and other universities, see G. C. Boyce, *The English-German Nation in the University of Paris during the Middle Ages* (Bruges, 1927), and P. Kilbre, *The Nations in Mediaeval Universities* (Cambridge, Mass., 1948); as to the primary materials, see

Chartularium Universitatis Parisiensis, ed. by H. Denifle and E. Chatelain (since 1889), and *Auctarium Chartularii Universitatis Parisiensis*, ed. by H. Denifle and E. Chatelain (since 1893)].

J. B. Mullinger, *University of Cambridge from the Earliest Times to the Royal Injunction of 1535*, vol. I (Cambridge, 1873), is still the standard work on Cambridge.

Oxford can be best studied in Rashdall, supplemented, as in the case of Cambridge, by the history of the several colleges. [Compare C. E. Mallet, *A History of the University of Oxford*, vol. I: *The Mediaeval University and the Colleges Founded in the Middle Ages* (London and New York, 1924); see also the highly illuminating articles published in 1949 by F. M. Powicke in his collection *Ways of Medieval Life and Thought* (London, n.d.): "Bologna, Paris, Oxford: Three studia generalia" (pp. 149–179); "Some problems in the history of the medieval university" (pp. 180–197); "The medieval university in Church and society" (pp. 198–212); "Oxford" (pp. 213–229)].

[On the cultural background of the era in which the earliest universities originated, see C. H. Haskins, *The Renaissance of the Twelfth Century* (Cambridge, Mass., 1928); G. Paré, A. Brunet, and P. Tremblay, *La renaissance du XIIe siècle: Les écoles et l'enseignement* (Paris and Ottawa, 1933); P. Delhaye, "L'organisation scolaire au XIIe siècle," *Traditio*, V (1947), 211–268; E. Panofsky, "Renaissance and renascences," *Kenyon Review*,

VI (1944), 201–234; W. K. Ferguson, *The Renaissance in Historical Thought* (Boston, 1948), esp. ch. XI].

II

The most useful general work on the content of mediaeval learning is Henry Osborn Taylor, *The Mediaeval Mind* [4th ed., 2 vols. (Cambridge, Mass., 1925, and later reprints); see also F. B. Artz, *The Mind of the Middle Ages, A.D. 200–1500: A Historical Survey*, 2nd ed. (New York, 1954), with an excellent bibliography; on the conditions of learning during the earlier Middle Ages, see M. L. W. Laistner, *Thought and Letters in Western Europe, A.D. 500–900*, 2nd ed. (London, 1957)].

This may be supplemented by R. L. Poole, *Illustrations of the History of Mediaeval Thought and Learning*, 2nd ed. (London, 1920); M. Grabmann, *Geschichte der scholastischen Methode*, 2 vols. (Freiburg, 1909–1911); [see now also Grabmann, *Mittelalterliches Geistesleben; Abhandlungen zur Geschichte der Scholastik und Mystik*, 3 vols. (Munich, 1926–1956); M. de Wulf, *History of Mediaeval Philosophy*, vol. I, trans. from the 6th French ed. by E. C. Messenger (New York, 1952); E. Gilson, *History of Christian Philosophy in the Middle Ages* (New York, 1955)].

J. E. Sandys, *A History of Classical Scholarship*, vol. I, 3rd ed. (Cambridge, 1921); [G. Highet, *The Classical Tradition* (New York and London, 1949); R. R. Bolgar, *The Classical Heritage and Its Beneficiaries* (Cambridge, 1954)].

L. Thorndike, *History of Magic and Experimental Science*, 6 vols. (New York, 1923–1941); P. Duhem, *Le système du monde de Platon à Copernic*, 5 vols. Paris, 1913–1917); C. H. Haskins, *Studies in the History of Mediaeval Science*, [2nd ed. (Cambridge, Mass., 1927); G. Sarton, *Introduction to the History of Science*, 3 vols. (Baltimore, 1927–1948); A. C. Crombie, *Augustine to Galileo: The History of Science, A.D. 400–1650* (London, 1952)].

Compare the standard histories on mathematics, medicine, and law [e.g., D. E. Smith, *History of Mathematics* (Boston and New York, 1923–1925); D. Riesman, *The Story of Medicine in the Middle Ages* (New York, 1936); A. Castiglioni, *A History of Medicine* (New York, 1941); P. Vinogradoff, *Roman Law in the Middle Ages*, 2nd ed. (Oxford, 1929); Q. Breen, "The twelfth-century revival of the Roman Law," *Oregon Law Review*, XXIV (1944–1945), 244–287]. See the more special literature in L. J. Paetow's *Guide to the Study of Medieval History*, including Paetow's own study of *The Arts Course at Medieval Universities with Special Reference to Grammar and Rhetoric* (Urbana, Ill., 1910), and his edition and English translation of Henri d'Andeli's *La bataille des VII arts* (Berkeley, Cal., 1914).

For a sample of Abelard's *Sic et Non*, see A. O. Norton, *Readings*, pp. 19–25. Abelard's method can be followed further in the logical writings edited for the first time by B. Geyer, *Peter Abaelards philosophische Schrif-*

ten, 4 vols. (Münster, 1919–1933); [see also J. G. Sikes, *Peter Abailard* (Cambridge, 1932)].

[On John of Salisbury see now the standard biography by C. C. J. Webb (London, 1932), and H. Liebeschuetz, *Medieval Humanism in the Life and Writings of John of Salisbury* (London, 1950)].

[On the *dictatores* discussed in this chapter by Haskins, see his own fundamental article, "The early 'artes dictandi' in Italy," *Studies in Mediaeval Culture* (Oxford, 1929), pp. 170–192; see also H. G. Richardson, "Letters of the Oxford dictatores," *Oxford Historical Society*, n.s., V (1942), 329–450; H. Wieruszowski, "Ars dictaminis in the time of Dante," *Medievalia et Humanistica*, I (1943), 95–108; Wieruszowski, "Arezzo as a center of learning and letters in the thirteenth century," *Traditio*, IX (1953), 321–391].

The best account of the class-rooms of a mediaeval university is F. Cavazza, *Le scuole dell' antico studio bolognese* (Milan, 1896).

Robert de Sorbon's *De conscientia* is edited by F. Chambon (Paris, 1903).

[On the question of the teaching licenses, see G. Post, "Alexander III, the 'licentia docendi,' and the rise of the universities," *C. H. Haskins Anniversary Essays* (Boston, 1929), pp. 255–277; G. L. Haskins, "The University of Oxford and the 'ius docendi,'" *English Historical Review*, LVI (1941), 281–292. On the problem of tuition charges, see G. Post, "Masters' salaries and student-fees in the mediaeval universities," *Speculum*, VII (1932), 181–198; G. Post, K. Giocarinis and R. Kay, "The medieval heritage of a humanistic ideal: 'scientia donum Dei est, unde vendi non potest,' " *Traditio*, XI (1955), 195–234].

III

Brief sketches of student-life will be found in the last chapter of Rashdall [2nd ed., III, 339–464], and in the little volume of R. S. Rait, *Life in the Mediaeval University* (Cambridge, 1912); [see also U. T. Holmes, *Daily Living in the Twelfth Century: Based on the Observations of Alexander Neckam in London and Paris* (Madison, Wis., 1952)].

In the text I have drawn freely from an article of my own on student letters (*American Historical Review*, III (1898), 203–229), and from one on the Paris sermons (*ibid.*, X (1904), 1–27); [both articles were revised and expanded in C. H. Haskins, *Studies in Mediaeval Culture* (Oxford, 1929), pp. 1–71, with detailed references to the sources used].

John of Garlande's *Dictionary* will be found most conveniently in T. Wright, *A Volume of Vocabularies*, vol. I (London, 1857), 120–138; John also wrote a *Morale Scolarium* [which has been edited, with an English paraphrase, by L. J. Paetow (Berkeley, Cal., 1927)].

The *Manuale Scholarium* has been translated and annotated by R. F. Seybolt (Cambridge, Mass., 1921). *Statuta vel Precepta Scolarium* have been edited by

M. Weingart (Metten, 1894), and by P. Bahlmann in *Mitteilungen der Gesellschaft für deutsche Erziehungs- und Schulgeschichte*, III (1893), 129–145. [Compare Haskins' own article on "Manuals for students" in his *Studies in Mediaeval Culture*, pp. 72–91].

A good discussion of mediaeval manuals of manners is by S. Glixelli, "Les contenances de table," *Romania*, XLVII (1921), pp. 1–40.

The best single collection of Goliardic verse is J. A. Schmeller, *Carmina Burana* (Breslau, 1894); [a new critical edition of *Carmina Burana* (text and commentaries) was started by A. Hilka and O. Schumann (Heidelberg, 1930)]. The best translations are those of J. A. Symonds, *Wine, Women, and Song* (London, 1884; many later reprints); [see now also the translations by H. Waddell, *Mediaeval Latin Lyrics*, 5th ed. (London, 1948, and later reprints), and by F. Whicher, *The Goliard Poets* (Cambridge, Mass., 1949)].

Two poets have been individualized, the Primate by L. Delisle and W. Meyer, the Archpoet by B. Schmeidler and M. Manitius. On the origin of the word "Goliardi," see J. W. Thompson, in *Studies in Philology*, XX (1923), 83–98, published by the University of North Carolina.

For an introduction to the vast literature of Goliardic poetry, see Paetow's *Guide* [2nd ed., pp. 484 f., 489–493]; P. S. Allen, in *Modern Philology*, V, 423–476, and VI, 3–43 (1907 and 1909); [see also P. S. Allen, *Medieval Latin Lyrics* (Chicago, 1931)]; and H. Süssmilch, *Die lateinische Vagantenpoesie des 12. und 13. Jahrhunderts als Kulturerscheinung* (Leipzig, 1917). [See also M. Manitius, *Geschichte der lateinischen Literatur des Mittelalters*, vol. III (Munich, 1931), esp. pp. 963–984; H. Waddell, *The Wandering Scholars*, 7th ed. (London, 1934, and later reprints); F. J. E. Raby, *A History of Secular Latin Poetry in the Middle Ages*, vol. II (Oxford, 1934); J. de Ghellinck, *L'essor de la littérature latine au XIIe siècle* (Brussels and Paris, 1946), esp. vol. II, 270–284; on the Primate of Orleans and the Archpoet, see also K. Langosch, *Hymnen und Vagantenlieder* (Basel, 1954), esp. pp. 292–340].

[See also the following recent publications: *The Septicentennial Celebration of the Founding of the Sorbonne College in the University of Paris* (Chapel Hill, N.C., 1953); P. Kibre, "Scholarly Privileges: Their Roman Origins and Medieval Expressions," *American Historical Review*, LIX (1954), 543–567; F. Pegues, "Royal Support of Students in the Thirteenth Century," *Speculum*, XXXI (1956), 454–462.]

INDEX

INDEX